Introductions in Feminist Theology

2

Editorial Committee

Mary Grey
Lisa Isherwood
Catherine Norris
Janet Wootton

Sheffield Academic Press

Introducing Body Theology

Lisa Isherwood and
Elizabeth Stuart

Copyright © 1998 Sheffield Academic Press

Published by Sheffield Academic Press Ltd
Mansion House
19 Kingfield Road
Sheffield, S11 9AS
England

Printed on acid-free paper in Great Britain
by The Cromwell Press
Trowbridge, Wiltshire

British Library Cataloguing in Publication Data

A catalogue record for this book is available
from the British Library

ISBN 1-85075-995-2

Table of Contents

Editors' Preface

The Britain and Ireland School Of Feminist Theology is committed to
providing various platforms for feminist theology; currently summer
schools, academic courses and publications produced by Sheffield Academic Press. These include the *Journal of Feminist Theology*, several
monographs[1] and most recently the *Introductions...* series, in which this is
the third title. The first title *Introducing Feminist Theology* (Lisa Isherwood
and Dorothea McEwan, Sheffield: Sheffield Academic Press, 1993) was
well-received and provided a solid resource at an academic level for
those new to the subject. Its success provided the idea for a series of
brief and relatively inexpensive books introducing aspects of feminist
theology presented by specialists, with the aim of providing reliable
guides to the history of thinking in each area, the current issues and
debates, and possible future development. Readability and accessibility
are the characteristics of the series, and the range of material and
diversity of authors provide a useful collection of views on different
aspects of feminist theology. The authors intend to challenge patriarchal
theology and to suggest liberating alternatives to it. We hope that
readers will find themselves empowered by these presentations and
energised to re-think traditional theological categories and ideas.

In presenting *Introducing Body Theology*, the third in the series, Lisa
Isherwood and Elizabeth Stuart have a very different task from Rose-
mary Radford Ruether, whose *Introducing Feminist Redemption* appears
at the same time. While redemption as a theological concept has a
long history and is well understood, body theology only surfaced very

---

1.   Melissa Raphael, *Thealogy and Embodiment: The Post-Patriarchal Reconstruction
of Female Sacrality*; Linda Hogan, *From Women's Experience to Feminist Theology*; Lisa
Isherwood and Dorothea McEwan (eds.), *An A–Z of Feminist Theology*.

recently and is still not a well-defined area of study; like its subject matter, it is difficult to pin down, departs from the ideal norm, shape-shifts and resists attempts to be systematically encoded. The authors, both known for their interest in body-based politics, trace the deleterious effects of the dualism that has persistently down-graded bodies (especially womens') in the interests of freeing minds (mens') to strive for abstraction, a process that underlies Christianity's ambivalence towards validating the body. They open up the subject of body-centred theology to encompass cosmology, ecology, sexuality, ethics and immortality and suggest areas of future exploration. There is something very exciting about their approach, and about the feeling that by engaging with a comparatively new discipline we are actively helping to develop it. In view of the massive media interest in health, fitness, size, ability and every aspect of bodiliness, where the provenance of received opinion about what is 'good' (sporty, thin, energetic) and what 'bad' (inactive, fat, quiet) escapes unquestioned, it is vital that the political/ theological givens that underpin such assumptions are revealed and that alternatives are proposed and examined. The authors of *Introducing Body Theology* do both with an understanding of the issues at stake and a sympathy that comes from their experience of embodied being. Readers will be encouraged to do their own thinking along these lines and can hardly fail to work out their own body-positive theology. It has certainly been a stimulating book to edit.

Introduction

We feel it is necessary to make a couple of points clear before embarking on a book about the body. Our first break with tradition is that we take the female body as normative throughout this work. Although we consider the work of male writers we do so from the perspective of the female as normative. This is not simply to make a point about the exclusion to date of the female body in serious discourse, although we trust it does so, but because as women we feel able to speak about the female body and in so doing to show how powerful we experience such bodies to be. Of course, we acknowledge that even speaking about the female body as we do is only a partial knowing since we do not experience what it is for all women to have and be judged through the possession of their particular body. We are sited in a particular time and place and therefore have to treat with respect the testimony of those who inhabit other spaces.

The differences that a body-based theology can create have become apparent during the writing of this book. Having started from a roughly similar place we have found that our views have become quite diverse. This has meant that we have stuck to writing our own chapters instead of collaborating throughout—which was the original idea (Lisa wrote 1, 2 and 6; Liz wrote 3, 4 and 5—we have collaborated in the final chapter). We agree with most of what the other is saying but we hope an added pleasure in reading this book will be to play detective and decide where we substantially disagree with each other! We have learnt a lesson in this process and that is the strength in diversity that exists in body theology. We have also learnt that different views can coexist in a book without damage to its integrity.

There are, however, a number of things which as Christian feminist liberation theologians we agree upon and have at the heart of our theology:

1. Incarnation, by which we mean that which we call divine, is redeemingly present in and between people and nature. This incarnational nature of reality is revealed most fully in the person of Jesus.

2. Sin and redemption are not just metaphysical realities but lived in the here and now in the real lives of people.

3. Women's experience is not only important but central in the creation of theology. This experience is sited in the body which includes the mind. It is necessary to state this as we do not wish to be accused of reinstating the old chestnut that woman is most strongly body and her biology is her destiny.

The Body

A definition of the body as 'a solid state of matter' refers primarily to the 'the physical or material frame or structure of man [sic] or of any animal: the whole material organism viewed as an organic entity' (*Oxford English Dictionary*, 2nd edn, 1989). While the most precise meaning of *body* is, then, a living organism, the term can be used analogously for any solid: 'a separate portion of matter, large or small, a material thing; something that has physical existence and extension in space' (*OED*).

The body is deeply symbolic in human culture, the means by which and through which the person and the community express themselves. But exactly what the body symbolizes about human nature and community is a matter of constant debate. Sarah Coakley has drawn attention to some contemporary understandings of the body.

> In materialist philosophy of mind...the 'body' may be everything else except the brain; in feminist analysis of pornography and cultural manipulation it represents the female that males seek to control; in both Freudian and Foucaultian accounts of sexuality it becomes the site of either forbidden or condoned pleasures, rather than the more-or-less unconscious medium of all human existence; and in popular magazine discussions of slimming and fitness it still stands for the rebellious fleshiness that has to be controlled and subdued from some other place of surveillance (Coakley 1997: 6).

In an age when we can transplant blood and organs from one person to another in order to bring life; when people's bodies can be augmented by artificial means; when a person's sex can be altered; when beings can be cloned; when heterosexual and patriarchal understandings of the body are breaking down, issues of bodily identity worry us and yet in an age when aesthetics appears to have largely replaced metaphysics, the body seems to be all we have (even, as Coakley notes, as it disappears on the internet). The body matters and so it is little wonder that a distinctive genre of theology known as body theology has developed. But in truth Christian theology has always been an embodied theology rooted in creation, incarnation and resurrection, and sacrament. Christian theology has always applied both the *analogia entis* (analogy of being) and the *analogia fidei* (analogy of faith) to the body. The body is both the site and recipient of revelation.

Nevertheless, the body has caused many problems for Christian theologians over the centuries, not least when they have attempted to define what it actually is. Is the body merely flesh, does it carry within it this mysterious attribute called soul? What happens to the body after death? Which type of body is the nearest reflection of the divine likeness? These are not neutral questions asked by the simply curious, they are powerful because the answers dictated the way in which society defined itself.

The Christian Scriptures naturally have embodiment at their heart. From the moment when Mary agrees to give birth to a special child, bodies become sites of revelation and redemptive action. Jesus' mission is begun with touch, by water and by a dove. People are touched and healed, they are forgiven and healed. The dead are raised and a woman shows her love through anointing and massaging Jesus' feet. The life of Jesus as told by the evangelists is a very physical one; he was not a philosopher simply engaging the minds of people on his wanderings through the land. Here was a man who held people, threw things in anger, cursed things making them wither and cherished people back to life. Here was an incarnate/embodied being.

The importance of the body is taken up by Paul and it is no exaggeration to say that it is central to his theology. The body holds together all his key themes: we are delivered from the body of sin and death, the body of Christ saves us, the Church is his body on earth, his body in the eucharist sustains that community and it is in our body that we are brought to new life. It would be a mistake to see Paul's views of the body through Greek, and thus *dualistic*, eyes, that is, as separate from and inferior to, the spirit. What appear to be demeaning remarks about 'the flesh' are in fact simple observations about the fallible nature of human beings. However, at times 'being in the flesh' is merely a fact of life and at others it separates us from God and is incompatible with the Christian life. It seems that for Paul this did not have the anti-sensual/sexual connotations that it later came to have. For him being in the flesh meant relying on oneself or the law and not the power of God. There is some tension in his body theology of course since the body not only binds us to the rest of creation in a positive way but also, for Paul, to the fallen creation and so to sin and death. It is only through identification with Christ that we overcome our fallen state.

The tension that is evident in Paul has been played out in various ways through the history of Christianity although generally dualism has played more of a part in these interpretations than it ever did for Paul. For example the sensuousness of mediaeval Catholicism can be contrasted with the disciplined and cold approach of Protestantism. The mediaeval church believed that sanctity and sinfulness could literally be smelt, the sweet odour of sanctity versus the stench of sin. This was a time of relics, affective piety and devotion to various body parts of Jesus. There was emphasis on 'carnal knowing' which is well illustrated in the writings of the women mystics who loved Jesus passionately and expressed it with their bodies. This was a time of sensuous engagement with the divine, but it has to be noted that this was not always a body-positive time.

The Protestant Reformation actually shifted the emphasis from sensual engagement with God to mental communion through the word of the gospels. Emphasis was placed on the mind's ability to grasp the revelation of God and the body was placed in a strait-jacket to keep it from the worst excesses of Catholic piety and superstition. The Reformation encouraged people to experience their minds as separate from and superior to their bodies which in turn led to an individualistic view of life. This was because salvation depended on mental, cognitive connection with God and a healthy distrust of things of the world, indeed the world itself. However, as we shall see, such generalizations hide diverse and complex attitudes to the body in every age.

There continue to be many reflections upon the relative importance of the body of the individual and that of the body of Christ or/and the Church. In this book we attempt to weave together some strands of body theology using the method of feminist liberation theology. Our approach, while attempting to be enlightening by bringing together and reflecting upon much of the body theology to date, is not uncritical. Indeed, we hope that this critical guide will raise further questions and help produce more radical maps. We actually hold no fixed notions of where body theology will lead. The body in all its majesty and mystery is full of surprises. Enjoy the journey!

Chapter One

Why Body Theology?

There are many answers to the question 'Why body theology?' The secular response may well be 'why indeed?' with a conclusion that there is no point, no need or no way! Secular feminists, however, would loudly disagree with 'no point, no need' since they understand the body as the site of female oppression. Nevertheless, most would discourage theological effort since many view religions, with the possible exception of goddess religion, as patriarchal beyond redemption. Many Christians may acknowledge the importance of the body in theology although traditionally it has been viewed as something to be overcome in order to receive the joys of heaven. This is paradoxical since probably the most important article of Christian faith is that God became man. It is therefore hard to believe that the body has been so despised, rather than loved and celebrated, by generations of Christians.

Christian feminists, like our secular sisters, realize that the bodies of women have been expected to carry a great weight under patriarchal theology. From the moment that we are asked to believe that Eve was a rib removed from the side of Adam we understand that theology is based in the body and we are at a disadvantage! If the Genesis story merely laid out a 'scientific act of creation' it would be significant enough, but it is a myth that has set the theological agenda for women and our bodies. An agenda that is still impacting on us today. The rib, once removed, becomes an object, an 'other', quite separate from God's original creation, man. This is to be the role of woman in religion and theology, to act as the 'other', the outsider, to the holy trinity of man, God and church. Man is the norm of creation and woman never quite measures up; all that is unique about her is seen as somehow defective and suspect. She is taught to mistrust herself, particularly the knowledge that she gains through her 'guts', her body knowing. Man will define who woman is, he is given the divine sanction to name her (Gen. 2.23-24) and he will dictate how she is to see herself and the world.

Admittedly there is another creation myth (Gen. 1.26-27) in which God creates man and woman in his image simultaneously, but this has not been the dominant story throughout the history of Christianity. Even had it been, there were still problems for women. Eve, the mother of all the living, let her children down badly. She was tempted by the serpent and ate of the forbidden fruit of the tree of knowledge thus causing the Fall of the human race. A Fall that had bodily consequences as it brought suffering and torment into this previously beautiful creation. Woman will have pain in childbirth and man will toil at earth that is cursed. The serpent is reduced to going on its belly and the man and woman will find no peace together. Each bears the consequences in their bodies and the earth itself suffers at its very core for the sin of Eve.

Christianity tells us that it took the incarnation of God, the divine becoming flesh, to overcome the great devastation wrought by Eve. It was the body of Christ that took away the sins of the world. It is the body of Christ that brings redemption to the world and to the individual believer. The same body that many of the faithful consider themselves consuming in the Eucharist. This is a very earthy, fleshy, physical way to connect with one's God and should set the pattern for a positive approach to the body. As we will come to understand, an incarnational faith is no guarantee that bodies will be treated with respect, given dignity or seen as sources of divine revelation.

Christology has developed along dualistic lines that owe more to Greek philosophy than to the Jewish origins of the Jesus movement. We hear of how Paul converted the Hellenistic world but we hear less of how the original Jewish movement had to adapt to have a hearing. The thought patterns of Plato and Aristotle influenced the growing movement. This led to a God and Messiah removed from the world in a way that would have been difficult for Judaism to imagine. The gods of the Greek pantheon replaced, to a certain extent, the God of history, the one who walked with his people through the desert and made his ways known in the history of his people. This movement away from the created order is the great paradox of incarnational faith. It has set in place a hierarchy with God and spirit presiding and the various manifestations of the flesh in descending order. Women, and nature itself, are at the bottom since man has claimed for himself rationality and spirituality which are nearer to divinity than are matter and the flesh. Dualism has led to the notion that all that is truly worthy lies beyond the body and ultimately in heaven. Christians must try to dwell spiritually within a physical body which has traditionally meant removing oneself as far as possible from the reality of that body.

Abusive 'Fathers'?

Despite the constant emphasis on incarnation the history of the church shows how dualism has remained a strong theme. Sometimes this has gone too far even for the church's liking and the movements which advocate these extreme views have been declared heretical. The Gnostics provide a good example of where dualistic thinking can lead. They viewed material creation as evil and therefore some advocated an ascetic life while others felt total abandonment to the world was the best course of action. Some groups believed that it was with the creation of woman that evil entered the world and therefore women were to be avoided. They thought there was a divine spark which resided in humans and had to be released through knowledge. Similarly the Manicheans and Albigensians speak of the light trapped in the body and in need of release. Both advocated ascetic lifestyles as a way of controlling the dark forces at work in the world and the body. For the Albigensians the only hell was the imprisonment of the spirit in the body.

Although these groups and others were declared heretical the established church nonetheless shared many of their ideas. The way that monasticism developed in the west can hardly be seen as body-affirming and this-world positive. Rather, it graphically illustrates the strength of the underlying dualistic thinking that has come to dominate Christianity. Many monastic rules and practices reflect a terrible fear and loathing of the flesh which often manifested in abuse of the body in order to achieve a spiritual perfection. The monastery was seen by many generations of Christians as the place of moral perfection, a sanitized place where the soul could gain ascendency over the unruly body. The history of western monasticism stands as a testament to the desire to split body and soul, while many of the activities indulged in show to what extent the body was despised. Flagellation, lack of sleep and very restricted food intake are hardly ways of celebrating the body and regarding it as a place of divine revelation. In short, these are bizarre practices for those who declare an incarnational faith. Of course, these practices did not just spring up, but had a theological tradition behind them. The Church Fathers have greatly influenced the development of the theology of the body. Unfortunately, in the main, their influence has not been positive. A snapshot of some of their most negative views will illustrate this point. (The approach of the fathers is dealt with in more detail later.) Jerome warned very strongly against touch, particularly against touching women. He advised male virgins to wrap their hands in robes before giving the sign of peace in case the touch of a woman made them lustful (*Pseudo-Clement Epistles*). Jerome was also anxious about taste and so food had to be carefully monitored as nothing excited passion as much as undigested food and hiccough. He warned women not to press their teeth together or speak with a lisp as this would lead to adultery of the tongue. Tertullian feared sight was a pathway to lust and impressed on women that it was their responsibility not to provide too much visual stimulation. Hot baths were advised against by many of the Fathers since anything hot led to passion; spicy food, for example, was not to be taken on any account. Ambrose advised against smelling too sweet as this could lead to lust. He also thought that one was known for one's deeds by one's smell! All the senses were snares waiting to entrap the aspiring soul.

The Fathers did acknowledge that sex could be pleasurable but they also thought it was degrading and disgusting. Lust was the enemy for both sexes but the Fathers had quite distinct advice for men and women. The division between the sexes was thought also to signify the division between the physical and the spiritual. Men represented the spiritual and therefore had to subdue and dominate the physical. Men's rugged voices and shaggy eyebrows were given as demonstrations of their innate ability to dominate and therefore rule. Every act of intercourse was seen as the spirit (man) becoming entrapped in sinful flesh (woman) and women were viewed as insatiable and innate temptresses. Men who came under their power were believed to lose their rationality, spirituality and masculinity. The Fathers, while seeing women as inferior, also feared them. Women's bodies were thought to possess all kinds of power, their hair or their menstrual blood could turn wine sour, corrode iron or cause dogs to go rabid. This power to corrupt had to be tightly controlled if women were to approach holiness. A woman's world was very confined and many women were advised to remain indoors. How they ate, slept, bathed and spoke were prescribed as well as what was modest for a Christian woman to wear.

Much of the advice borders on the perverse. Karen Armstrong is forthright when she says that the advice of the Fathers at times reads like a sexual assault on women (Armstrong 1986). Jerome was impressed with the way that women would make themselves repulsive for God, their self-mutilation delighted him. Anorexia, masochism and degrading behaviour were ways that the Fathers felt made women holy. While men's bodies were also treated with disdain it is certainly the case that the bodies of women received the most abuse from the Fathers. The Council of Elvira devoted 26 of its 81 canons to greater control of women's bodies while only 12 regulated the sexual/body behaviour of men. The perceived naturalness, indeed 'divineness', of these regulations serves to establish a social structure that literally embodies and legitimates the dominant values of a group. In this way 'the biological differences between male and female bodies become symbolic of other cultural boundaries and categories' (Power 1995: 8). By legislating for control of bodies power is gained over the whole cultural structure that springs up, particularly kinship systems and economics. A case can be made to show that the church has always had an interest in such control as just one aspect of its allegiance to patriarchy.

It is very difficult to assess to what degree Christianity has influenced the development of a patriarchal culture and therefore attitudes to the body. It may be that the culture of patriarchy has affected the development of Christianity. What we are able to say is that our culture holds patriarchal views of the body and our church reflects all these negative traits. Christianity and patriarchy are highly compatible bed-fellows. This means that as feminist liberation theologians we have to address the reality of the imprisonment of the body under these systems and look for a way to break free from the crushing embrace of patriarchy. Theology has been slow to address many of the issues around the body and feminist theology is a long way behind its secular sisters. Therefore we need to listen and assess whether our own discipline has the capacity to argue for the same freedoms. Is theology, and particularly Christian theology, moral enough to lift all the negative injunctions against the body and allow celebration to take the place of guilt and repression?

The Challenge

It is not surprising that the main challenge to the myths surrounding the body and the culture that springs from them should come from those who are least well served by the culture. Trusting their own experience,

women and gay men were the first in our recent history to challenge
centuries of negative mythology perpetuated about them. They let their
own experience speak and stood up against stereotypes. It could be
argued they had little choice since society often punishes people who do
not 'do' their gender the 'right' way. Both groups came to understand
that the way society viewed their bodies was the site of their oppression.
As de Beauvoir realized a woman is not born she is made, and her
making is in order to support the male dominated status quo, she is
made into what is useful. Body politics challenge the so-called 'natural
laws' and of course thereby challenge the theological framework that
underpins western society. Although God plays no part in our secular
society it has to be acknowledged that these 'natural laws' were originally seen as such because they supposedly reflect God's design for the
universe. For example, the inequality between the sexes has been and
still is attributed to the notion of complementarity which can be derived
from a patriarchal reading of the Genesis myth. Eve is taken from the
side of Adam thereby signalling that the two halves need to be made
whole once more. There is, of course, an agenda of inequality at work
here since the man is seen as possessing the 'better half' of human attributes. Woman being a derivative of man can never expect to possess the
original, good qualities to the same extent. This is not just a view that
can be lifted from the Hebrew Scriptures, it is also there in what at first
seems a very positive statement for women—the Pauline injunction
regarding equality in Christ (Gal. 3.28). On closer inspection we see
that what is actually assumed is that woman disappears, the rib slots
neatly back into place and the male image of God is left as he was first
placed on this earth. In Christ the breach that occurred in Genesis is
healed and man once again shines in unitary glory (Børresen 1995: 62).
Presumably it is not beyond the bounds of speculation to assume that at
the *eschaton* woman will cease to exist but until that time she will be
judged against an androcentric norm. Børresen argues that Christ had to
be incarnate as a male if he was to represent perfect humanity, such is
the weight of patriarchal ideology (1995: 190). It would have been
inconceivable to the Fathers that a woman might be the divine incarnate. Indeed, for them it was often hard to imagine that woman could
be holy. This is a trend which started in Ephesians where we are told
that woman's salvational equality is gained by achieving Christ-like
maleness (Eph. 4.13). It was picked up and carried on with vigour,
Tertullian imagining that resurrected women would be a mixture of

angels and men. Jerome thought that if a woman wished to serve Christ she had to give up being a woman (*Exposition of the Gospel of Luke* 10.161) while Ambrose added that a believing woman does indeed progress to complete manhood (*Regula Episcopi*, Preface).

The present Pope prefers to refer to complementarity as 'different but equal'. However, the double speak is revealed when we realize that those who are 'different' are excluded from many of the activities that the 'norm' takes for granted, for example, priesthood. Complementarity divides the sexes in a way that can never lead to equality or indeed full humanity for either sex. It assumes that neither sex is complete without the attributes of the other. Apart from dividing people within themselves it is also a homophobic way of seeing the world. Those in same-sex relationships can never, under this system, find full humanity. Complementarity is put to more sinister use by the religious right in the United States. The bodies of women and the interpretation put on them are used by this group to advance a christo-fascist societal agenda. The Moral Majority advanced a so-called 'Family Protection Act' in 1991 which called for lack of contraceptive choice for women as well as a total ban on abortion, divorce and sex education for women. The same document declares that it is the duty of Christian women (the assumption is that these women are white) to stay at home and breed as many Christian children as possible to halt the tide of minorities who breed at 'epidemic' proportions. The language is emotive, and it is meant to be. The consequences of women not following their 'divine and natural' role are spelled out very clearly:

> millions would be put out of work, multiplying minorities would create ugly turbulence, smaller tax bases would diminish the military's nuclear weapons stock pile and a shrinking army would not be able to deter potential Soviet expansion (Faludi 1992: 53).

The problem that feminist theologians face is highlighted in the above. For secular feminists and gay theorists what has just been described is merely wrong. They point to psychology and the social sciences to show that the notion of complementarity has a political agenda which is not based on fact and therefore no longer needs to be served. Feminist theologians do not simply have to deconstruct patriarchal society but the patriarchal God as well.

Many of the most pressing questions raised by secular feminism are in the area of the body-self and sexuality and as we have seen these areas have been the most closely supervised and restricted by the male guardians of the Christian tradition. Adrienne Rich poses the question clearly:

> In arguing that we have by no means yet explored or understood our biological grounding, the miracle and paradox of the female body and its spiritual and political meaning, I am really asking whether women can not begin, at last, to think through the body, to connect what has been so cruelly disorganised (1977: 192).

This is a fundamental question for incarnational theology and actually sets the scene for body theology which creates theology through the body and not about the body. Working through the body is a way of ensuring that theories do not get written on the bodies of 'others' who then become marginalized and objects of control. It is also a way of deconstructing the concept of truth that Christianity has used to hold so many falsehoods in place. Once one moves from the notion that there is absolute truth into which the bodies of people have to fit, the way is open to begin questioning and we soon realize that truth is not the issue in relation to prescriptions about the body, but power. Christian history shows us the extent to which power has been exerted over bodies in the name of divine truth and the crippling results. If the body is given the space and power to speak what will be the consequences for both the body and theology?

Feminism, by emphasizing the centrality of women's experience has given it a power that it has to date never known. The Women's Movement claimed that women had the right, based on their own experience, to define their own lives. This is a revolution under patriarchal Christianity which claims the right of definition for itself and the male God. Slowly women are coming to understand what it means to be human in a way no longer defined by the dominant culture—to no longer be the 'other'. Irigaray challenges de Beauvoir's definition of woman as the Other seeing even this 'Otherness' as constructed by patriarchy. To begin a critique of the dominant culture from the place of otherness is nonetheless to place oneself within that culture. Women therefore need to find a way to be 'where they are' undefined and free. This may be a mere dream for as we will see even our body-knowing bears the mark of patriarchy.

It can be argued that both the history and the destiny of women are written on their bodies. Feminism acknowledges this possibility and therefore sees the body as the site not only of oppression but of rebellion. One such area where we have learnt our place by practical enactment and therefore may stage our rebellion by acting differently, is sexuality. Irigaray encourages us to find a language that is continuous with our desire as this may be the only way to represent woman. Woman who, according to her, represents a sex which cannot even be thought since so much thinking is itself phallocentric; woman, who represents a linguistic absence, needs to struggle for a body presence. The language that is needed is that of the body, in this way the flesh becomes Word. The female body offers a new paradigm, a new knowledge, one that challenges the traditional Word. It places embodied subjectivity at the heart of knowing and declares invalid 'objective absolute rationality' which has been the 'norm' within patriarchal mythology.

Who Defines Female Sexual Desire?

Female desire has been dictated by both male desire and male fear. The way the bodies of women are used, abused and 'supposed to be' carries a political agenda. The sexual power agenda has been brilliantly highlighted in the work of both Sheila Jeffreys (1990) and Margaret Jackson (1994) who show how women have been coopted into their own oppression through sexuality. Jackson shows how traditional views of sexuality, that is missionary position sexual intercourse between married people, have a dominance agenda. She claims that 'the art of love was about securing the consent of women to male dominance and female submission by eroticising it as "natural"' (1994: 185). Her survey highlights how women have to be 'educated' into this submission by being taught how to behave and what to feel during coitus. Havelock Ellis the renowned sexologist, who we may well name as the patron saint of rapists, advised that a woman may say no but that is only modesty and it is the man's job to overcome the woman. He counselled that it was fine to have sex even when the woman was protesting as this was merely conscious resistance while her unconscious instinct would be to want intercourse. He was not alone in arguing for missionary position sex as the most natural (many churches also pursued this line of thinking) as it combined the male desire to conquer with the female desire to be conquered: he wished to possess her and she was grateful to him for doing so (Jackson 1994: 168). Women's pleasure, he told aspiring Romeos, is very like pain and since their genitals are less sensitive than men's, pain is in fact an added bonus.

The women who resisted this script were seen as unnatural and placed in dysfunctional categories—frigid, lesbian, spinster, prude. The 'authorities' on these illnesses were in no doubt that power was the issue. Wilheim Stekl, a recognized authority on frigidity, viewed it as resistance to male power. To allow oneself to be aroused by a man meant that one acknowledged being conquered which is the natural way to be. Orgasm overcomes the final barriers of resistance and so the 'unnatural' woman tries to avoid it. Her

> instinct to dominate is stronger than her sex hunger; she wants, while being subjected, to remain unconquered... Poor woman: she does not know that it is precisely by renouncing the strongest element of her personality that she preserves the essence of femininity (Haine quoted in Jackson 1994: 175).

Sexologists at the early part of this century were interested in educating the vagina and by so doing naturalizing the claims they made about sex, power, dominance and, at times, violence. One or two did acknowledge the existence and potential of the clitoris but it was generally felt that its role in coitus, for women of the white races, was inconsequential (Jackson 1994: 156). Sexism and racism are once again convenient partners in debates about what is natural. The more mature sexual response was from the vagina, an idea that Freud developed in his misguided pondering on the nature of women. The 'fact' that the clitoris was differently placed in white and black women explained the more infantile, wild and animalistic responses of black women during coitus; responses that would be quite unsuitable for a well brought up white lady! Marie Stopes received the wrath of the establishment when her book *Married Love* advised these young ladies of the possibility of sexual fulfilment. Instead of rejoicing in the new possibilities for mutual pleasure, one member of the House of Lords complained: 'If you create these vampire women you will rear a race of effeminate men' (Jackson 1994: 137). It is clear that what occurred in the bedroom carried implications far beyond, even to the Empire perhaps which could not, after all, be ruled by a bunch of effeminate men!

Although women these days are encouraged to be more active sexually, Jeffreys reminds us that the sexual revolution has not freed women. For the most part what is defined as liberated still carries a male and patriarchal agenda. She views the sexual revolution with some regret since it masks the dominance agenda that was so blatant in the 1950s. Freudian therapists and others in the 1950s were quite clear that once a woman acknowledged she was conquered through intercourse she would no longer nag or attempt to assert her will in domestic affairs (Jeffreys 1990: 3). Christian marriage manuals advised husbands to 'take' their wives by force in order to assert their headship in Christ. The wife, we are told, would be excited by this approach. Undoubtedly being taken by such a 'muscular Christian' was good for the soul.

Jeffreys' survey of the sex manuals of the 1970s and 1980s reveals the unsurprising fact that they carry a male agenda. *The Joy of Sex* sold more than most and was hailed as the liberated person's guide to sexual plea-sure. However, it contains strange advice. Women are encouraged to delight in any fantasy that their men may have, however degrading, and are warned that failure to act out these fantasies may end in the divorce courts (Jeffreys 1990: 117). All the activities assume an active role for men and the goal of each activity is penetration. Two messages are con-veyed very strongly by such manuals, one is that women who are 'liberated' are most pleasing to their men and secondly that penetration is what really constitutes sex. What they fail to take into account is the research of those such as Shere Hite who have found that a very high percentage of women, some 86 percent, do not reach orgasm through penetrative sex (1993). Further research and common sense also tells us that the majority of women do not find it a turn on to be degraded and abused (Borrowdale 1991). What is most worrying about the sexual revolution is that it has simply made women more available on male terms. One's position in society is conveyed via body learning and we are still being encouraged to learn the age old patriarchal narrative, 'be fucked, be joyful and be silent'. Feminist sexual practice not only requires a critique of the way that sex is used in a patriarchal society, but also needs commitment to exploring a model of mutuality between equals. We have to find ways to make mutuality sexy in order to replace the eroticization of our domination and in so doing overcome the alienation we suffer from ourselves.

Many feminists in the 1970s, Jeffreys amongst them, became political lesbians. That is, they understood the danger involved in the patriarchal construction of sexuality and attempted to place themselves outside it. In her book, *The Lesbian Heresy* (1994) Jeffreys examines how the hey-day of lesbian feminism is in decline. Younger lesbians have, she claims, abandoned the political idealism of their fore-sisters and bought into the male construction of sexuality as dominance/submission, so prevalent in the male gay scene. Lesbian porn and the use of women in lesbian escort agencies coupled with a reintroduction of role-play signals to Jeffreys that her hopes and dreams are being sold out. Instead of being the place in which women could find a language continuous with their desire, same-sex relationships are being coopted into the dominant myth without its obvious societal benefits. The role-playing is not of the kind that Joan Nestle could describe as revolutionary, where the butch was not a heterosexual replica but a woman who took responsibility in the world. A major part of this responsibility was to give sexual pleasure to women. As Nestle points out, in the 1950s having the courage to arouse another woman became a political act (Seidman 1992: 116). It was a way of being sexual outside boundaries and prescriptions of power, to hear a woman through her body, to take notice of female desire. Further, it was a challenge to traditional understanding since the butch, while the sexual agggressor in terms of being the one who made the running sexually, was concerned with her partner's pleasure more than with her own. In a further twist the femme was the one who provided economically since the butch often found it hard to get work—women in suits were not that employable in the 1950s. To take notice of female desire in this way was, and could still be, revolutionary.

Monique Wittig is more hopeful than Jeffreys about the current state of lesbian identity which she sees as shaking gender 'as stable political categories' (Butler 1990: 113). For her a lesbian is not a woman since a woman, under patriarchy, is that which is in binary opposition to man. A lesbian wishes no relation with a man and therefore is placed outside the narrow definitions of sex and gender, refusing to be the 'other'. She is in a place where she can create a new reality if she understands her radical potential. It is this lost potential that Jeffreys mourns. By taking on definitions such as 'butch daddy' or 'lesbian boy' the radical nature of lesbian identity is lost in normative sexual domination. The power imbalance that such categories suggest bear no resemblance to feminist ideals. From these categories often spring sado-masochistic practices and other objectifying rituals. The connection between our most intimate body experiences and the way in which we function in the world is a dynamic and complex one. It can be argued that sado-masochism is both the result of and the perpetuator of an alienated society. A society, that under the influence of Christianity and its self denying philosophy, has made mutual and equal pleasure a difficult goal. Alice Miller (1988) clearly shows how we are brought up in an sado-masochistic society, that is one in which the equal satisfaction of needs is not a possibility, nor desired if the status quo is to be maintained. In order that patriarchal society exists at all there has to be an unequal power relation; the child learns this pattern in the home and the wife has it reinforced in the marital bed. We are, it seems, made susceptible to patriarchy at our mother's knee, in the bosom of our Christian families and in our most intimate acts. It is this susceptibility that lesbian feminism felt it could immunize us against and it is this lost chance that Jeffreys and others mourn when they view the introduction of patriarchal patterns into the lesbian lifestyle. Empowerment experienced through intimate equality they felt could just change the world.

Of course not all women adopt lesbianism as a political stance but most feminists do understand that:

> No act of penetration takes place in isolation. Each takes place in a system of relationships that is male supremacy. As no individual woman can be liberated under male supremacy, so no act of penetration can escape its function and its symbolic power (quoted in Griffin *et al.* 1994: 79).

If we are in doubt about the symbolic power of the penis and penetration we only have to cast a glance at British law and popular culture. It is only penetration by a penis that makes a woman an adulteress, the most vile and violent sexual assault serious enough to be a rape, that counts as real sex and, in Christianity, consummates marriages. The ability to penetrate makes a boy into a man, with all the attendant privileges, and the power they feel can turn men into rapists. The language that describes penetration also gives a hint as to its symbolic function. A woman is fucked, screwed, poked, taken, had, given one. This is not the language of equality. When such a fleeting act holds so much power, to define it needs to be critiqued.

Marilyn Frye suggests that women need to remain wild and free, to be undomesticated by the power inherent in phallocentric sex. In order to achieve this women have to find a place of strength in themselves, a place that she calls virginity. The virgin she claims is never captured or subdued (quoted in Griffin *et al.* 1994: 178). Frye advocates virgin heterosexuality while others suggest 'fucking with gender' which implies the possibility of doing sex in a way that actively disrupts normative definitions of sex and gender. What is being challenged by this approach is the notion that there is anything fundamentally natural in sexual expression. There is nothing that is essentially male or female that has to be underpinned through prescribed physical activities. Anything that transcends the rigid boundaries of gendered sexuality is to be celebrated. There is nothing here about shaggy eyebrows making one dominant or reproductive sex being the only excusable kind. This is a celebration of embodiment beyond all definitions, enjoying a body for its own sake. It is an attempt to allow people to be framed by their bodies and not by culture or doctrine. Women often discipline themselves to fit a model of sexuality which prioritizes male desire and defines their own fulfilment in terms of love and giving pleasure and this self-giving by women is encouraged in Christianity. The appropriation of women's bodies is what is being rebelled against. It is, of course, a very privileged rebellion since many women cannot afford to remove themselves from the social construction of hetero-patriarchy. If we are in doubt about this we only have to examine the figures related to AIDS amongst women in Africa. These women know the dangers of sex with their infected husbands but are unable to move outside the cultural construction of sexuality, they simply cannot afford to. Battered wives who remain in the relationship also highlight the extent to which women will deny their own body selves under the weight of the patriarchal myth. Patriarchal sexuality is the reality of most women's lives whether it is to their advantage or not.

Many women feel it is to their advantage while others believe it is God given. In 1995 a group of Tory women called for a fidelity bonus! Their commitment to monogamy, the great backbone of the patriarchal myth, is absolute. Just how important an issue this is can be understood when we examine what people believe are the consequences of, for example, single motherhood. We are constantly told that juvenile crime is the fault of the single mother, the woman who leaves her man and drains the state while letting her children run riot. This is far from the truth but it highlights a deeply ingrained prejudice, one that has been set in place by religion and culture. The free woman has to be the evil, or at best, the dangerous woman. From the Hebrew Scriptures (e.g. Tamar, Rahab) to recent Tory diatribes we see the woman outside marriage viewed with suspicion and blamed for some social ill.

Monogamous marriage for women has been a central part of most western religions and cultures. On close inspection of its origin this appears to support the issue of ownership rather than one of romantic love and commitment. Proving the fatherhood of children is important under patriarchy and the economic and ownership systems that it spawns. Monogamous marriage also fits well with complementarity since it brings the two halves of humanity back together in a tightly regulated system. Monogamy, which assumes a close pair-bonding, has consequences that reach into wider society. Women who live outside this institution are largely ignored as real people in society as a whole. Even matters such as credit status can still be a difficult matter if one is not seen to have the backing of a man regardless of one's own financial situation. The perceived security that women feel in monogamous relationships also tends to make them give priority to that relationship and this does not always act in their interests. Women's friendships are vital in the struggle for liberation but the notion of monogamy keeps women divided. It not only makes them place their energies into their one primary relationship it also make them view each other as rivals. The idea that one has to keep one's man fuels many industries in the western world that have severe consequences for women's bodies. The ethic of service that we mentioned in relation to the prioritization of male sexual desire is also in full swing here. Women will go through many kinds of physical discomfort and even mutilation in order to serve the needs of men. Super models have ribs removed to ensure that the clothes look good and Melissa Raphael tells us that the calorie intake on an average diet is less than that received at Auschwitz (1996). Women do not enjoy diets nor do they relish liposuction or 'corrective surgery', so why do they do it?

Monogamy also harnesses women's labour in a way that serves the system. The age old debate about the cash value of women's house-wifely work is still current. The way in which women's labour is abused under this system is best illustrated in the Third World although it is by no means inappropriate to consider it in relation to our own setting. Women do 80 per cent of the work and own less than 2 per cent of the profits. It is too simplistic to suggest that if women left the institution of marriage they would correct this imbalance, but it is fair to say that the institution adds to the problem. The bodies of women are used as cheap labour outside the home or free labour within it, the demands placed on them by marriage enable this to happen. To understand this fully we need to think globally and not simply through middle-class British eyes.

Heterosexuality and monogamy as practised under patriarchy keep the hierarchy in place. It is little wonder, therefore, that homosexuality is perceived as such a threat. Gay theorists have challenged the dominant discourse on many levels. However, much gay theology is still at the level of attempting to justify the right to live and find sexual expression. This is inevitable given the dualistic mindset and spiritual hierarchy that is in place within Christianity. There is a long way to go. Body theology is not concerned with justifying a gay lifestyle. What is far more interesting is how a gay lifestyle can inform the theological discourse and expand its boundaries.

By asking what a discourse *does*, rather than what it *says*, Foucault opens the way for a searching critique of society. The Christian discourse *says* that homosexual activity is wrong since it goes against the natural order set in place by God. Fiery rhetoric. What this discourse does is relegate more than 10 per cent of the human race to an inferior position in society and church—at times to a place of fear and often a place of limited human rights. So clearly, what it *does* in the light of a gospel of liberation, is wrong. If the weight of society in this matter is in doubt we only have to point to the closet. People do not put up with the discomfort of the closet because they are ashamed of who they are but rather because of the consequences of stepping outside. The existence of the closet is the result of a complex set of power relations. To come out is a dangerous thing to do even in these enlightened times. People in this country may no longer be sent to the stake or put in prison but they are abused and marginalized. Further, the out gay lifestyle becomes a convenient stage for heterosexual society to project its fantasies and anxieties. Therefore, 'coming out is an act of freedom, then, not in the sense of liberation but in the sense of resistance' (Halperin 1995: 30). The resistance is to the narrow definition of self and the injustices that society imposes. However, it is also a creative process, in refusing to allow society to be comfortable with its definitions, one refuses to be an essence and becomes a 'strategic possibility' (Foucault, quoted in Halperin 1995: 75). Of course, this has difficulties for the traditional Christian who may believe that people do have an essence rooted in the image of God. Further, that male and female essences are differently prescribed by God. Gay resistance then, as here described, challenges Christianity on two levels, that of justice and in relation to the 'essence' of God and creation.

Gay lifestyle also challenges Christian ethics. Foucault talks of 'desexualization' which means taking sexual pleasure away from the normal forms of expression. In this way he claims we liberate our desire and create new pleasures. This is a philosophical activity as it opens up new ways of being, by decentering the subject and fragmenting personal identity.

> The shattering force of intense bodily pleasure detached from its exclusive localization in the genitals and regionalised through various zones of

the body, decenters the subject and disarticulates the psychic and bodily integrity of the self to which a sexual identity has become attached. By shattering the subject of sexuality, queer sex opens up the possibility for the cultivation of a more impersonal self, a self that can function as the substance of ongoing ethical elaboration—and thus as the site of future transformations' (Halperin 1995: 97).

Before women claim we have already been decentred enough through our sexuality we should remember that this is a male argument. It is, therefore, encouraging to see a male discourse acknowledge the power of the penis to localize and control as well as to define the identity of those in possession and reception of it. It is perhaps inevitable that such a recognization had to come from a gay man who has less to lose through his vision. It is, of course, a challenge to traditional Christian ethics which would not encourage such liberty nor feel comfortable with the use of the whole body for sexual pleasure dissociated from commitment and reproduction. The hope that the future should be queer, that people explore their bodies beyond normative sexual patterns, is not a hope easily shared by mainline Christianity! Hope for a queer future is not purely hedonistic, it is also political. Pleasure will carry people beyond narrow confines and into an open future, one that has not yet been thought but may have been felt.

Is it possible for an eschatological religion like Christianity to have such an open future? Indeed, can a religion that has such a fixed image of God at its heart even dare to explore this open future in the way described? Traditionally Christianity has been a religion of 'givens', of absolutes and this makes it very difficult to progress. However, despite the difficulty, history shows just how it can and has changed. Body politics have exposed the underlying power games at work in sexuality and society and by so doing have become a source of inspiration and liberation for many. Christianity is an incarnational religion that claims to set captives free, it tells us it is a religion of liberation. Yet it underpins many of the restrictive practices that body politics expose. In some cases Christianity has been the instigator of these practices because of its dualistic vision of the world.

The Christian faith has had to face many challenges in its long history and, despite its rhetoric, has not remained completely untouched by the challenge. The questions being posed in our time are to do with the body, that of the world as well as the individual. Can body politics ever become body theology in a truly radical and transforming way? This might mean for example, that the Christian religion attempt to sustain a

Christology that is continuous with female desire. That it risk taking the bodies of women seriously as sites of revelation in the creation of theology. That it stand the challenge to the image of God that queer theory and the 'real' existence of women throws up. That it develop a sexual ethic that takes seriously the desire of all and integrates it into a mutual and freeing celebration of embodiment. Christianity will also be required to liberate itself from the traditional patterns of marriage and monogamy that it has preached since these may not be liberating patterns for all. It will have to develop and promote patterns of relating that encourage people to express freedom and eroticize their equality.

So why body theology? The Christian faith tells us that redemption is brought through the incarnation of God. A redemption that could not be wished or just thought, even by God herself, she had to be enfleshed. Therefore, it can be argued that until the body is liberated from the patriarchal ties that bind it, many of which have been set in place by Christianity, creation will never understand the truly liberating power of incarnation.

Chapter Two

Method in Body Theology

It is one thing to say that body theology is the way forward and quite another to view it as a possibility within the Christian tradition. Until recently there has been no method available that allowed for the theological valuing of bodily experience. Traditional Christian theology, based as it is on dualistic assumptions, has always viewed the body as less important and more prone to sin than the mind. Theology, therefore, had to spring from reason and the spirit if it were to hold any credibility. By suggesting that theology can spring from the body there is no wish to say that it bypasses reason but rather that reason and feeling need to be reconnected. Body theology holds out the hope of healing the cruel rupture that patriarchal thinking has introduced into theology; it attempts to put the body, mind and emotions back together in order to see anew the glory and goodness of all of creation.

Scene Shifting and Shaping

Three very significant moves in the theological scene have made the process of body theology 'thinkable'. These are process thought, liberation theology and feminist theology. Together they have destabilized the dualistic hierarchy that is at the heart of patriarchal thinking and its body-subordinating attitudes. In their own ways these movements have critiqued the dominant notion that it is thinking alone that legitimizes and confirms man as the pinnacle of creation. 'I think therefore I am' can no longer go unchallenged or be assumed to underpin western philosophy but rather is seen as highlighting the fact that we have not moved beyond the pre-Christian Greek division of the world. This division into good and bad, black and white, mind and body, human and animal is at the heart of the antagonisms and destructive patterns of western life. We hope that an incarnational religion would wish to get beyond notions that were stuck in the Greek pantheon, but we acknowledge that it has been slow to do so.

Process thought, as advocated by Alfred North Whitehead, helps to undermine dualistic thinking. Heavily influenced by evolutionary theory Whitehead expounded a 'vision of reality' that saw the world as ever becoming through relationship. Evolution is possible because of the intimate relating of many aspects in the world, the interplay of which cause the next step in the process. Therefore, the very nature of the world shows that it is not dualistic but relational and so for Whitehead the highest achievement for humankind is to develop empathetic feeling rather than objective rationality (Whitehead 1929). All that is worth knowing is found in the relation and this is sited in the body, the emotions and the empathetic mind. We do not have to retreat from the world in order to understand it we have to move more feelingly toward it. We would like to argue that this is best done through the body, that is through the combination and connection of senses and mind with neither having priority but both aiming for understanding through feeling.

Whitehead claims that energy which can be scientifically observed in the world is in fact the 'emotional intensity entertained in life' (1938: 232). It is this emotional intensity (energy) that fuels both the cosmic drive of evolution and the individual drive for goals. Therefore, although we are a distinctive part of the created order we are not detached from the rest of the cosmos. Further, we will only really understand our true destiny when we realize that we are co-creators of the universe (Pittinger 1979: 10). We cannot merely think our way into this kind of intimate relationship as our mind alone will not take us there. This, of course, challenges the Cartesian and Greek philosophical tradition that assured us that the head knowledge made us comfortingly distinct from the rest of the created order and would ensure that the future was safe. There is no such arrogance or safety in the process model. All things are changing but not with a divine hand guiding it to the glories of heaven, the process is as yet undecided and we are the ones who create the future. Therefore searching for absolutes is a mistake even in matters of religion since the reality is the process and this will not be fossilized. This is not to say that there is no meaning in life; in fact his view places greater responsibility on each decision since they all matter in creating a future that we all share for better or worse with no external agent to redeem us if it all goes horribly wrong. The way to chart this uncertain future is by looking for patterns rather than absolute truths and the place to begin is in our experience. Experience mediated through and by the body. Therefore it can be argued that the body is central in the unfolding of process thought. This may not have been an insight that Whitehead made explicit but it can nevertheless be claimed. It also has to be said that Whitehead and his followers were not too aware of half the human race—women.

An evolutionary approach allows us to see the world as unfolding rather than moving from perfection to corruption. God is also unfolding since the deity cannot be disconnected from the process. Whitehead says of the divine:

> He does not create the world, He saves it, or more accurately, He is the poet of the world, with tender patience leading it by His vision of truth, beauty and goodness (1929: 346).

This God is echoed in Revelation as the one who makes all things new (Rev. 21.5), the God of creative movement. He is not the one who decides the rules before the game is even played and hands out penalty cards to those who interpret the rules differently. Since our natures are fluid it would be unwise to declare that God is static as this would face us with an insurmountable problem, how can we relate? Traditionally it has been the static and unchanging nature of God that proves his divinity and our changing natures that underline our sinfulness but this can no longer be seen as the case. Whitehead claims that we experience the relation between God and the universe as far too intimate to even argue for a God who is unable to relate due to a difference in essence. For Whitehead it is love that sustains both the process and the relationship. He says that the origins of Christianity show that:

> love neither rules, nor is it unmoved; also it is a little oblivious to morals. It does not look to the future, for it finds its own reward in the immediate present (1929: 349).

The God of Jesus was not interested in unchanging moral absolutes but in the unfolding process of love. (This can be seen in his disregard for the law and his concern for the physical needs of people, e.g., Mt. 12.1-8). This highlights the vulnerability of the divine and the importance of relationship on which love depends. The infinity of God is not a supernatural attribute but rather the divine capacity for love. Therefore the divine does not burst into the world in cosmic splendour through unususal acts but rather unfolds through love and intimacy. Although Whitehead did not emphasize the role of the body in this it is obvious that we do not experience this degree of intimacy through thought alone, we have to connect with others and through them with God who is in the intimate process. The body then is not to be tamed and repressed, but freed in order to move on to explore new ways of loving intimately. Pittinger claims that Jesus moved on in love and became the living Christ without ceasing to be the man of Nazareth (1979: 109). In other words he was a man in time and space, enfleshed and engaged with life and it was this which made it possible for him to enter more fully into the process of the divine. In the same way our physicality allows us the experience to relate lovingly and enter the process of divine becoming.

Process thought enables us to free ourselves from traditional notions of original sin. Nothing was ever perfect, but rather all the created order is in a state of becoming. This means that no part of creation can be scapegoated for sin which is good news for both women and the body. Further, the dualism which underpins these traditional beliefs is absent and so there is no spiritual hierarchy that has to be aspired to. The stuff of the universe is all that is necessary for the becoming of God. To remove oneself from that reality would be to deny the creative potential of the divine in relation. It can be argued by using the insights of process thought that the body in relation is the site of divine becoming. Process thought places God back in history in a more intimate way than even the Hebrew Scriptures did. History is also written on the body, and by the body, therefore the God of process thought is moving in the divine history of the body. God unfolds both in the bodies of individuals and the cosmos creating an intimate, interdependent and co-creative trinity. Therefore, to try and remove oneself from the body by dwelling in some spiritual realm would be the greatest denial of God and divine potential.

Process thought places God back in history and liberation theologies give direction to that divine potential. That is, the embodied God begins to articulate the desire for liberation felt in concrete situations; the call for justice takes on a real face. Until the 1960s the dominant theological view in the Roman Catholic Church was that society could not be changed by the efforts of human and political activity. This was underpinned by the doctrine of original sin and the Pauline dictate about the willing spirit and the weak flesh. All human efforts were seen as intrinsically flawed and therefore limited. Further, it could be argued, and often was, that suffering in this life led to reward in the next and so one should be resigned to one's place in the scheme of things. Hierarchy has always sat well with the Christian religion!

There were, however, signs of disquiet in European theology, with it being suggested that people had the potential to transcend themselves if placed in the right conditions for growth, that is, if injustice were fought against. The Latin American Catholic bishops reflected on this at a conference at Medellin in 1968 and challenged the situations of injustice that they saw in their countries. There was a realization that theology, in attempting to answer questions about God, has to understand the way the world works since the God questions spring from this world. Leonardo Boff is amongst those who encouraged theologians to stop thinking of the world as something to be prayed for or removed from and to see it as something that can be changed. For liberation theology the reality of God in flesh shows that history matters and that Jesus attempted to influence the course of history through his interventions in the lives of people. He was not just a 'sayer'; he was a 'doer' and this is the meaning of salvation that we 'do' many acts of justice in order to create the kingdom on earth.

Contemplation is at the heart of liberation theology but it is contemplation that begins in the lives of people and not merely reflection on the divine. Further, this reflection must lead to action. Central to liberation theology is the understanding that sin is not a metaphysical reality but rather consists in injustices that are perpetuated by people. Contemplation is not only to help us to see the injustice but to enable us to imagine ways of ending it. There is a very solid biblical base to this optimistic view and it is that God created all things and saw they were good (Gen. 1.31). Further, Jesus encouraged us to do things for one another and assured us that we would do greater things than he did. Gutierrez recommends that the optimism held by liberation theologians should not spill over into an idealized picture of the group it is serving, the poor in the case of Latin America. He suggests that we should be committed to a group not because we believe them to hold all the virtues *par excellence* but because justice demands it and because God is good (Isherwood and McEwan 1993: 75). A slightly different emphasis here might suggest that we will not know what God is until we, through the practice of justice which requires listening, actually hear God as being in the lives of the oppressed. This sounds a rather large task especially when we realize the amount of injustice in the world. It requires us to declare our preference in order to save our sanity; we are unable to save the whole world and so need to decide where our energies will be directed. Liberation method asks that we acknowledge the universal love of God but decide which corner we will fight in. This has meant that we now have a range of liberation theologies which far from being fragmented are using the same method to address the multiple array of oppression and injustices that people create.

All liberation theologies are calling the church to respond in a positive manner to the oppressed; though the church has at times been seen in the role of the oppressor particularly in matters of sexuality and gender. Liberation theology demands that the churches grow with the world and remain fixed in a fossilized state relying on received wisdom rather than God revealed in the process. Churches are still trying to maintain a hierarchy based on 'say-so', power-over, and are not trusting the spirit rising from the lives of the people of God and shaping a co-creative future. The churches generally speaking are not happy with this message as they still like to cling to hierarchy and power, and even those that claim there is no power structure are not free of its curse. The Catholic Church is to a degree the most honest in this matter, as it has declared itself hierarchical by divine institution! (Gibellini 1987: 45). Therefore, according to its own logic, it can make oppressive and demeaning statements about the bodies of its followers with impunity, for example, about the lack of contraceptive choice, the intrinsic moral evil of homosexual practice and so on.

Liberation theology has of course challenged this situation no more so than in feminist theology. Feminist theology places experience at the heart of the creation of theology, not the experience of the ruling males but of the individual believer. This cuts hierarchy to the quick and demands that individual lives be seen and taken seriously in matters of religion. After all experience has always been at the heart of religious life, it is only when some declare their experience more valid than that of others and then codify it into absolutes that the spirit is no longer one of freedom and liberation. By objectifying what is really subjective, power is sought and gained.

The emphasis on experience in feminist liberation theology is very valuable for body theology. It enables us to take seriously the whole of the person since experience is not something that we have just in our heads. This poses a challenge to theology which has claimed to be based on rationality alone and has functioned in a dualistic way. The body in its entirety is the site of experience. Further, the body does not refer only to the white male elite body, it cannot be colonized in the same way as reason has been. The body is far more expansive and inclusive. By focusing on experience the body becomes the site of personal redemption and redemptive interdependence. A reality that is not in any way new or against the teaching of Jesus but rather revives a process that has been crushed under the weight of patriarchal power.

Learning to trust and value our own experience is not as easy as it may sound since for generations Christians have denied their own embodied feelings and attempted to achieve disembodied perfection. The biggest hurdle to overcome is that of dualistic thinking, the notion that we are somehow not really our bodies. We have to put to one side the idea that lurking deep within is the 'real' me and the body is a mere unruly covering for this reality. We also have to put to one side stereotypes and projections that have been placed on the body in the name of religion. Women understand this activity very clearly since we have been seen as either virgins or whores when in reality most of us are neither. We have to learn to stand our ground where our experience is concerned and no longer accept the 'received wisdom' since it carries an agenda that makes it far from wise.

Opening the way for personal experience once more to be at the centre of the creation of theology is both exciting and frightening. Experience is such a diverse matter that we suddenly face the fragmentation of theology, it becomes messy as it becomes the stuff of real lives. Theology can no longer shroud us in the comfort of eternal absolutes since experience is a changing and expanding thing. There is an open future of challenge, the challenge of facing diversity rather than fitting into neat prearranged categories. Those who believed they held the power suddenly realize that they do not, but rather that power lies between people and within them as they strive for justice.

Beginning theological reflection from the concrete stuff of people's lives and not from some lofty contemplation of an Almighty Absolute is a revolution. Actually placing what we feel and experience in our everyday lives at the heart of how we begin to understand God is a reversal of traditional theological method. This 'theology from below', makes sense in an incarnational religion. Where else would we start the search for the incarnate God but in the stuff of the world. This method developed by liberation theology allows body theology to encourage an embrace of the created order. Body theology is able to allow the body and its experiences to be a site of revelation.

Critics of this method suggest that at best, or worst, we are left with a purely subjective set of ideas that are open to self-indulgent narrowness of thought and application. So can experience-based theology have universal validity? We first need to ask if it should have. Traditional theology has for too long declared that the reasoning of a limited number of men has some universal and divine truth. The methods of process and liberation theology would not wish to repeat that grave and power-laden mistake. However, both are also anxious not to fall into the trap of total relativism. Understood in the right way experiential/embodied knowing is neither self-indulgent nor narrow. Certainly it is true that all experiences are both expanding but also limited, they allow us to see things that we may have had no previous knowledge of but also they are mediated by our own place, time and incarnation. It could well be argued that all experience is culturally dictated and so can never be a force for driving us to expanded understanding and progress. However, the history of experience does not seem to bear this out, experiences do change people who in turn change society. There are many fundamental assumptions that underpin all experience and perhaps the first step is to actually name these and then consider them in the light of continuing experience.

Experience and interpretation are inextricably linked but feminist method does not wish to view these activities in a hierarchical way. The experience is as valid and important as the reflection and interpretation, in other words the interpretation is as embodied as the experience itself. We should not split experience and interpretation and fall into the trap of cold, harsh, universally applicable objectivity, that god of truth that disregards all but itself. Experience, to be rightly understood, also has to be seen as including relationality: We do not experience in a vacuum, nor should we 'think' our way to isolationism. We are related to the things that we experience. It is this relatedness that is the most exciting challenge in embodied thinking; we are never at liberty to remove our experience from that of others. Our experience often calls us forth in relation and it is this that enables us to deepen our thinking and acting in the world. The power of relation does not allow our thinking to detach itself from the world. Objectivity enables us to have elaborate theories which 'make sense' but are often devastating, while embodied thinking can never do this as we cannot detach ourselves from how our decisions 'feel', what their lived consequences will be.

From Theory to Application

Several theologians have begun their theology by looking at the consequences in their own lives if they took tradition seriously. One such is Virginia Mollenkott (1993) who poses the question:

> So how does a fundamentalist who believes she is essentially and totally depraved become transformed into a person who knows she is an innocent spiritual being who is temporarily having human experiences? (1993: 16)

The reason for her feeling of depravity was her lesbianism and the way to her feeling of 'spiritual innocence' was through her own experience, a small amount of which she describes as mystical but the large part of which was extremely 'this worldly'. She, like hundreds of others, sacrificed her sexuality to her spirituality at great cost to her sense of well being and identity. Therefore, hers is a journey of self-acceptance and the drawing together of sexuality and spirituality from the starting point of a fundamentalist. Any movement under those constraints is to be applauded but will naturally have limited outcomes. Although it should not be underestimated just what a step it is to practise one's sexuality without guilt under those circumstances.

Mollenkott asserts that the Ultimate is at the core of everything and everyone and despite our difficulties in recognizing this in others in this life we will all rejoice in our connections eternally. It is our alienated ego that makes us act badly and the power of the Holy Spirit that corrects this imbalance. This dualistic thinking underpins all her work although she claims that the body is important as the colleague of her soul. However, even the way she writes, referring to Self with a capital, implies that something which is not the body is the true her and the eternal and holy part. Life is a battle to lower ego-actions and raise Holy Spirit inspired actions (1993: 18). The heart of her theology is the notion that we are really spiritual beings having human experiences. This, however, falls down when she talks about justice-seeking. Injustice springs from alienated egos and the work for justice has to be underpinned with the knowledge that at 'a deeper place' everything is already right and 'salvation is complete' (1993: 22). However, she still argues for justice-seeking spirituality and even calls it sensuous in the sense that it is embodied and physical. The point of getting involved in justice-seeking does not seem to be entirely for the benefit of the world since she believes everything will be fine in the end, but rather if one does not: 'I will miss the blessing of playing my position on a team in a universal game in which everybody wins' (1993: 25). The body is the vehicle through which the Holy Spirit works to bring about change and so people need to integrate their feelings in order to make the Holy Spirit more welcome.

Mollenkott considers homophobia to be a projection of the alienated ego on to others and therefore sees it as dysfunctional as well as destructive of others. She, like Comstock (1993) argues from a biblical base and shows the array of interpretations that can be put on the material. Her conclusion is that it is fine to be gay and the Holy Spirit can flow through gay people too. Her work is essential for those who are still struggling with personal experience versus Bible and tradition. However, she still holds dualistic attitudes and some of the assumptions that spring from them, for example, that everything is worked out according to God's plan despite our weak human efforts. While she has taken on the validity of personal experience and its ability to challenge tradition she has not really thought much further than the integration of sexual orientation and tradition. However, we are our bodies, not merely resident in them, and it may be the case that they are far more radical than Mollenkott gives them credit for.

Gradually theologians are being imaginative and at times daring with the new freedom that process and liberation method has given them. It seems that they were for a number of years pleased that these insights had come to light, but almost too shocked at the possible consequences of such thinking to stray far from the traditional patterns slightly modified by this new thinking. This simply highlights what has always been known, that practice speeds ahead both of theology and church reform. By understanding the potential that bodies hold for revelation and authority both theology and religion will have to run if they are to remain relevant by declaring Christ in the lived experience of real people not plastic saints. It can be strongly argued that by concentrating on experience people are moving nearer to Christ incarnate. Isn't it time that theology gave up the old dualistic hierarchies? It has abandoned the old world view that saw the created order divided into three—the underworld, the flat visible earth and the heavens above. Surely the divisions of the physical body were meant to represent and reflect this cosmic pattern, so why do we still hold fast to this when we are not naive enough to hold such a divided world view? Perhaps we have reached a new frontier and therefore need to consider our traditional doctrine in a new light. Incarnation may indeed be a reality that carries more within it then even the originators of the doctrine could imagine.

James Nelson places incarnation at the centre of his work in body theology. His understanding is that incarnation was not limited to the person of Jesus but is a present reality in the bodiliness of all people. This has implications for the way in which we understand the nature of theological reflection which can no longer begin with the abstract but must start with 'the bodily experiences of life' (Nelson 1988: 17)—all the bodily experiences of life and not just those that we can understand as 'spiritual'. As encouraging as this seems Nelson's work does not totally manage to eliminate dualism from within itself. This simply high-lights to what extent it is engrained in our society and our psyches. When a person who is conscious of the need to move from dualistic thinking still finds it hard to do so we are in trouble!

Nelson claims that when we feel awkward and embarrassed by our bodies and more concerned with so-called high spiritual matters, we lose the capacity for passionate caring which he sees as the central task of the Christian life (1992a: 23). We somehow begin to think that we are not bodies but simply have bodies and they are of less importance than souls. It is from this mindset that we can harm both ourselves and others believing that in some way the essential bit of us will benefit from the rigours that the body is made to endure. This is a very unhealthy and fragmented way to deal with our lived reality. One of the most 'ground-ing' realities for Nelson is the realization that sexuality is not of our lower natures but in fact points us to the essential nature of God, which is relationship. Generations of Christians have dealt with vexed ques-tions about the place of sex within the Christian life and have relegated it to the outer limits of real life in the hope that they could forget about it. Nelson asserts that sexuality is a basic dimension of our personhood and therefore highlights the extent to which we are relational creatures. He concludes that we can find God in that relationship. Certainly his basic motivation is correct but it is not always the case that sexuality is relational; many women report that they do not even feel acknowledged as present when having sex with partners. If this can be reported during consensual sex how much more is it the case in acts of violence? In fairness to Nelson he speaks of authentic relationships and connections but he does not fully deal with the reasons behind the lack of relationship. It could be argued that this can be laid as much at the door of pure selfishness as at that of Christianity. If a culture has been affected by a mindset that devalues sexuality and women is it any wonder that we have problems looking at one another and acknowledging the presence of the other in acts that still trigger strangely ambiguous feelings in the majority of Christians. The notion is still strong that sex is an inferior action in which God can have little part; as Luther put it in a more liberal statement, God winks at sex! Nelson is a long way from this view seeing all bodies as in essence sexed bodies and therefore sex as part of the material from which we gain our understanding of God.

There is a certain sensitivity in Nelson's understanding of sexual expression that is heartening. He is aware that what he calls the 'genital-ization' of sex has made it performance-orientated and has heightened the dominant/aggressive image of sexual expression in men (1988: 67). Interestingly he also links this with insistence on virginity for women, noting that the inexperienced woman may be more easily controlled and patterned according to her partner's needs. This may help male insecurity but it also fuels male domination and so is an issue that needs to be dealt with from an incarnational point of view. What is called for is not just an understanding that these problems exist and a plea that Christian men resist the temptations of this kind of sexual construction, but a radical rethink on the nature of sexuality and its expression. This is happening outside Christianity while the churches seem to be becoming more and more entrenched in traditional views that feed the dominance/submission model.

Nelson argues that the whole of the body should be viewed as the source of sexual pleasure and far from running from it we should embrace it as a source of revelation. It is alienation from the body that makes us lack sensitivity and move towards control, both of ourselves and others (1988: 43). This is not free enough if we are to engage with the created order through a process model in which God is constantly revealed. Far from restricting the body we need to be as imaginative with it and the pleasure it gives us as we are able. Incarnational theology beckons us to find God in the here and now, in the material grittiness of everyday life and experience; this takes imagination! Imagination to turn even the worst situations into empowering experiences without running to a place of safety, that is to metaphysics and dualistic thought. The Hebrew Scriptures warn us that a people without imagination shall perish and this is abundantly true if what we see is what we get, if there is no get out clause like heaven and hell. Nelson makes the point clearly that 'in a world that does not really honour matter but cheapens it, in a culture that does not love the body, but uses it, belief in God's incarnation is counter-cultural stuff' (1992a: 195). By use of the body he is referring to capitalist exploitation as much as to sexual exploitation but it is sad to note that the churches are slow to pick up on either point but will nod more smilingly in the direction of a rethink of work conditions than on a new sexual ethic. For example, they are still slow to realize that the majority of marriages exploit women and their labour.

Nelson's fiery rhetoric is appealing but there is still a nagging doubt which is highlighted by his insistence that we meet Christ in our neighbour. This appears to harbour some dualistic thought. Admittedly Christ has moved nearer, out of the heavens and onto the earth among people, but there is still the notion that he is somehow there just waiting to be seen by those who have the correct vision. That Nelson thinks this way can be illustrated by his use of the term 'Christic reality', for him this reality already exists somewhere. The phrase 'Christic possibility' may be better since it does two things, it does not allow us for one moment to flee to the comfort of the 'already achieved' and it makes the here and now the place where we engage with redemptive work. In this way we are able to remain focused on the lives of people as the reality and the transforming relationality between them as the radical possibility. We need sensitivity to the fact that even talk of depth in this context leads us off in the wrong direction, it runs the risk of trivializing the 'surface', that is the reality of life and everyday experience. This smacks of dualism by any other name. It may be better to assert that there is intrinsic value in human life that does not need to look to God to be seen as such. Further, within that which is human there is the possibility to create that which we have called God. It is one possibility among many, there is also evil which some have called demonic. These are polarities and not dualities and both reside within the basic nature of things.

Where Nelson states that:

> God is uniquely known to us through human presence, and human presence is always embodied presence. Thus body language is inescapably the material of Christian theology, and bodies are always sexual bodies, and our sexuality is basic to our capacity to know and to experience God (1988: 36).

It may be worth suggesting that this continued incarnation of God is a possibility not a given. The incarnation is repeatable because it has been the lived reality of another human person, Jesus, but it has to be the lived reality of others before we can claim it is continuing. Nelson realizes that Jesus might have made decisions that would have led away from the Christic reality and he does acknowledge that we too have a choice in the way that we respond to others. There is nevertheless the assumption that God/Christ is already in the other person and so we are simply acknowledging that reality or ignoring it. There seems to be no acknowledgment in his thought of the creation of Christ between us through relation. This, of course, raises another serious question, whether we are responding to the person at all or to the 'Christ' as perceived within the person. This path runs the risk of devaluing the reality of the person and places them yet again in a hierarchical relationship under the shadow of the already-incarnate Christ. 'Not I but Christ who lives in me' is not a valid statement for those who take both process and liberation theology seriously. Christ is no longer a final 'Word', but rather an ongoing conversation with the whole body speaking.

Carter Heyward (1989) moves the debate on a pace or two with her discussion of the erotic and God as power in right relation. By 'the erotic' Heyward means the innate dynamic energy that is our deepest desire for union with others. It is our deepest passion that drives us to find justice. Rita Brock (1988) claims that it is this power that saves both us and Christ since it thrives on relationality and therefore saves Christ from the place of dominance in which he has been put by male theology! This erotic power challenges logic as the highest form of functioning; in fact it propels us beyond the narrow confines of reason to a place of sensual connection where things can be known for what they are. Heyward makes no distinction between the erotic and God thereby, one could argue, defining God as empowered physicality. So immediately we understand that God is not present as a given but made real in right relation. It has to be acknowledged that at times Heyward does speak as though God were a given although not in such a way that makes that God untouchable. In other words God can die, not as Jesus on the cross, but as the active and creative principle that is in the core of things. Heyward's God seems more partial than Nelson's in the sense that her deity is more reliant on our co-creative power to influence the world. Like Nelson, Heyward believes that it is in our embodiment that we connect/create this divine existence. Speaking as a feminist liberation theologian she is clear that our 'sensuality is a foundation for our authority' (1989: 93), which is consistent with the view that God may be seen as empowered physicality. However, she is equally aware that patriarchal culture has pulled us away from our true natures and this alienation has led to both a distortion of our selves and our idea of sensuality. She puts it as follows:

> to deny the sacred power of our embodied yearnings is to be pulled away from one another and hence from ourselves... To have our bodyselves trivialised and demeaned is to be snatched out of our senses and alienated from our erotic desires. This process of alienation from our sacred power produces antierotic (or pornographic) psyches and lives, in which our bodies and feelings can be jerked off by abusive power dynamics, coercion and dominantion (1989: 95).

Heyward is not alone in thinking that Christian theology has aided this process of alienation rather than celebrating the joyful release of the erotic in and between people and the created order. Through its dualistic and thus body-negative mindset Christianity has helped sustain a sado-masochistic society, one that literally depends for its survival on the suffering of others. This can be witnessed from the hearth to global economy and it is usually the bodies of women which bear the greatest burden. This sort of domination is only possible because we are alienated from our own erotic power and so the arrangement of sexuality in a society is extremely important to those who wish to keep the power. If we really celebrated the joy of embodiment we would literally be uncontrollable and where would advanced capitalism be then! Heyward highlights this by pointing out that while wife battering is seen as bad, gay sex which threatens male control is viewed as evil; while incest is a shame, lesbian mothers embody all kinds of evil forces and threaten the fabric of civilized society (1989: 55). It is possible to see her point. Power is sexualized and so the bodies of Christians have to be sites of resistance. However, they will have to resist their own tradition first and take authority within themselves rather than imagine it lies in a sysytem or even in an external Christ.

Heyward's Christology sustains her body-positive theology but of course strongly challenges traditional understandings. Incarnation is an ongoing process that is made visible in the embodied relationality between people. Heyward uses the story of the raising of Lazarus as an example; it was the commitment and passion of the women as well as the tears of relationality on the part of Jesus that brought about the radical transformation of death to life. Heyward rightly shows that this was no 'God on high' carrying out a magic trick for the assembled group. This story shows the transformative/redemptive power of relationality; a power that we all possess and need to trust ourselves to use if a truly redeemed world is to be the reality. Therefore, body theology has at stake a lot more than simply the bodies of 'witches and faggots' but rather 'the nature and destiny of God' (1989: 71). This is not to create a hierarchy here between the bodies of witches and faggots and the body of God but rather to highlight the complexity and enormity of the task and the stakes. We have to get the power relations right if the God of justice and compassion is to have life. Heyward acknowledges that we all suffer from some kind of power distortion and therefore places great hope on our ability to heal one another through the empowerment of touch. She calls for tender and urgent touching through which we 'journey together through places of brokenness and pain toward safety and tenderness' (1989: 104). This healing is not in a vacuum and it connects us more deeply with the pain of the world because our new sense of well being highlights more starkly the injustices that exist. In this way lovemaking is justice making as it fuels our indignation at the pain and exploitation of the bodies of others. Our own embodied experience of being brought to wholeness kindles both our imagination and our anger and we can no longer remain alienated from ourselves or the common humanity we share. Christian theology has encouraged only sterile touching, if any at all. Christian love is somehow portrayed as ethereal and 'otherworldly' but certainly not as passionate. Heyward is suggesting that we only begin to move towards the process of Christian love when we delight in our bodies and the bodies of others. It is through this delight that we learn to respect ourselves, others and the whole created order. Christianity, by placing bodily restrictions, has helped us to fear one another and this has led to a form of alienation that is most damaging—holy alienation. For Heyward alienation is contrary to the reality of incarnation.

Heyward does not wish to make any distinctions between sex, spirituality and God. She views all three as 'empowering sparks of ourselves in relation' (1989: 4). Real lovemaking is wrestling with the reality of justice making and she is aware that this does not have to take place in a monogamous relationship or even a long-term relationship. Indeed, it may be the case that the 'religious legality' of monogamy could actually blind people to making justice together. Heyward is totally convinced of the power of good sex to transform the world. It does this because it turns us into ourselves and beyond ourselves. In this way too it is the correct site for theological reflection. She states that it is no longer good enough for her to merely read and think her way through theological questions if she is to find God and justice. Heyward's method is truly body theology: She says:

> I had to make love
> and if I had not had a precious woman
> to caress my lusty flesh
> and bring me open not only to her
> but to myself and you
> I still would have had to find a way
> to enter more fully
> the warm   dark   moisture
> of One in whose hunger
> for survival and passion
> for friends   and movement
> for justice   and yearning
>   for touch and pleasure
>   we are becoming
>   ourselves (1989: 2).

Here she is not making a sentimental statement about the nature of sex between people but rather acknowledging and affirming the public and dynamic nature of private acts of love. It can be argued that women have to stop being objectified in their sexual selves and start to experience their bodies as strong, powerful, autonomous and creative. This is a task that will not be easy under patriarchy but, as we have shown, the future of God depends on it.

Naturally the stance taken by Nelson and Heyward finds no favour with much mainstream theology. Although many of the worst statements of the Fathers are no longer endorsed there is still not a body-praising attitude in much religion and theology. Much of the religious discourse is still about trying to save 'the young and the perverted' from themselves by advising self-control and more self-respect. Beverley Harrison challenges these views and turns them on their head by asserting that it is precisely the kind of objectification that we learn from fearing and subduing the body that leads to lack of self-respect and valuing of others. In short there is not too much sex around but rather not enough! The control ethic never actually succeeds in controlling our desire, it simply disconnects our desire from our self and thus makes us more able to objectify both self and others in our most intimate acts. Christianity has placed this control ethic in the area of sexuality and Harrison advocates it should be replaced by an ethic of play (1985: 150). It is with an attitude of playfulness that we will come to realize that our sense of self as civilized is not compromised by our passionate and sexual selves. Christianity needs to joyfully release sexuality from the bonds of marriage and procreation if people are to understand that it is sensuality that connects us to each other and the divine. Sensuality is the ground of our transaction with the world and the foundation of our creativity, it is 'our power to affect and to be affected'. If we deny it we are denying not only genital sexuality but our ability to be affected and thereby to make change. Harrison puts it powerfully when she says:

> All of us, then, literally call forth each other in relationship and our power of being and capacity to act emerges through our sensuous inter- action in relation (1985: 157).

We are called to change the world not through self-emptying sacrifice as with *agape*, but rather through mutual, interactive, self-affirming sensuous love. How far this is from the Christ of the power brokers and yet how close to the man of the gospels who sought relationality.

By way of observation and not criticism of the work of Heyward and Harrison it could be suggested that the self-affirmation that women are to adopt may be easier in lesbian relationships than under hetero-patri-archy. This is not to argue that lesbians are the saints of the feminist revolution, far from it, but rather that a woman-identified environment may be less affected by the worst excesses of patriarchy. (Sheila Jeffreys' laments are noted.) Indeed, it is a suggestion that Heyward herself makes, believing that same-sex relationships by their existence challenge the dominance/submission model, that is the norm. Of course separatism is not the only Christian option, male clerics tried it and look where it has got us! Rather I would like, with Charlotte Bunch, to define a lesbian as 'a woman whose sense of self and energies centre around women... She is important to herself' (1987: 162). This is revolutionary in a society that uses female energies in the service of male defined goals and it is a revolution that need not be confined to women who have sex with women. Indeed, it is a revolution that should be inspired by an incarnational theology in which the development of the self is seen as a holy task and not as self-indulgent or having an inflated sense of one's own worth.

The developments that have taken place in theology mean that the body has become a site of serious theological reflection and on going revelation. This seems to be wholly consistent with an incarnational religion. The implications of valuing the body and experience in this way are far reaching in theology, church structure and ethics. Difference will name itself with authority and the strangle hold of imperialistic centralization will have to be relieved. In this way the body of Christ will have more meaning as it will become a living and breathing reality of people striving to live justly—justice that has to be striven for in the concrete stuff of their lives not simply in neat theological declarations. Therefore, by its nature it will be a far more glorious tapestry of shade and vivid colour illustrating the unfolding of our divine becoming.

Chapter Three

A Difficult Relationship:
Christianity and the Body

Interest in the history of Christianity's relationship with the body has necessarily followed from the late twentieth-century western preoccupation with the body as a important site of intellectual analysis. Societies and cultures which are rooted in the Christian tradition have at least to take that tradition into account when wrestling with contemporary issues. Unfortunately the results of this interest, even from some theologians, have often been little more than distorting generalizations along the lines of 'Christianity has always subordinated the body to the soul' or 'Christianity has always preached hatred of the body'. Whilst it is possible to amass a collection of 'sound bites' from across the Christian centuries to support such claims, any attempt to examine the Christian tradition(s) in contextual depth undermines such easy generalizations and reveals a complex, constantly shifting relationship with the body which goes right back into the tips of Christianity's roots.

The Word and the Flesh: Bible and Body

One of the most oft repeated generalizations is that ancient Judaism had an entirely positive attitude to the body. This is true to some extent— there was in ancient Judaism none of the rigid dualism between body and soul, the human being seems to have been regarded as unitary nor was there any suggestion that sexuality was other than a God-given gift and an essential part of being human. The Song of Songs fairly pulsates between the covers of the Bible, offering a glorious celebration of human sexual desire and bodiliness for its own sake. Fertility is not a theme in this work. It is by no means clear that the couple are even married and certainly there is something subversive about the relationship which drives others to violence. It is the closest the Hebrew Scriptures ever come to presenting us with an equal and mutual relationship between a man and a woman. God's presence is identified in the closing section of the book as residing in the passion between the lovers.[1] Although it is quite customary these days for scholars to dismiss the ancient allegorical interpretation of this work as a love song between God and his people or Christ and his Church as a reflection of ancient discomfort with the body and sexual passion, we should remember what this allegorization did. It made God both the giver and receiver of embodied passion, eroticizing the covenant relationship in a manner that those prophets who used the marriage metaphor failed to do because at the heart of that metaphor was an assumption of inequality and violent domination and submission. Nevertheless it would be quite false to conclude that ancient Judaism never problematized the body. Even within the Song of Songs there is an awareness of the ambiguity of erotic love which is inspired by difference but which drives towards a merging which signals its own death. The equation of love and passion with death in 8.9 hints at this ambiguity.

It is in the biblical material usually ascribed to priests ('P'), particularly the book of Leviticus, that preoccupation with the body and particularly with what goes in and comes out of it is most obvious. The body is shown to be liable to pollution from various foods (Lev. 11) and from its own discharges and emissions (Lev. 12 and 15). Lack of bodily integrity whether caused deliberately (for example as part of mourning rituals) or congenital or the result of disease, also caused impurity (Lev. 19.27; 21.2 and 21.16-23). The blurring of boundaries, between species or between genders, through bodily activity was also regarded as being an unclean act (Lev. 18; 20.10-21). Israel was called by God to be a holy nation and this essentially involved being separated from other nations (Lev. 24b-26) with significant boundaries being vigorously policed.

The classic explanation for the priestly preoccupation with the body was provided by anthropologist Mary Douglas. She argued that the body often becomes the symbol of the social and religious structures to which it belongs and the anxieties of the society are played out on the human body. In the case of ancient Israel, 'The Israelites were always in

---

1. In 8.6 the term Šalhebetyā is used to describe the fire-like nature of the love between these people. It means 'a flame of yah' or 'Yahweh's flame'. At the very least a comparison is being made between their love and the fire of God, at most it is being claimed that the love they share is part of God's burning love. For a full theological analysis of the construction of desire in the song see Walton 1994.

their history a hard-pressed minority...The threatened boundaries of their body politics would be well mirrored in their care for the integrity, unity and purity of the physical body' (Douglas 1966: 124). So concern for bodily purity and integrity is a reaction against the threat to the unity and integrity of the body politic. Bodies which perform certain acts or bear certain marks which seem to symbolize the malaise of society are demonized and excluded. This is true not only in ancient Judaism but also in Christian history. The mediaeval creation of the 'leper', including the poor and heretics as well as the sick, and the irredeemable 'Sodomite' are both examples of creating 'bodies' to represent various threats to society, bodies which can then be punished and contained (Jordan 1997). Certainly, during the time that the priestly strand of the Hebrew Scriptures was being formed, Israel was in potentially fatal chaos following the exile and it is therefore understandable, following Douglas's theory, why the priests should have become preoccupied with bodily purity. But there are some flaws in the theory which are drawn out by Howard Eilberg-Schwartz, who points out that Douglas never explains why, in light of the fact that Israel was almost constantly under some sort of threat, preoccupation with the body appears to be largely confined to the priests (Eilberg-Schwartz 1997: 34-55). Nor does Douglas explain why discharges and emissions from the body were interpreted as threats to wholeness.

Eilberg-Schwartz offers an alternative analysis which is focused specifically on the priestly group. This group had to wrestle with some conflicting beliefs which clustered around the human body. The priests believed, on the one hand, that God had commanded human reproduction (Gen. 1.27) and made it an intrinsic part of his covenant with Abraham (Gen. 17.4-6). This is why this covenant is 'written' on the male reproductive organ. Indeed, Eilberg-Schwartz maintains that one of the priests' primary aims is to associate fertility (and hence God's chosen people) primarily with masculinity and an attempt is made to break the 'obvious' connection between women, fertility and reproduction by associating menstrual and birth blood with impurity and death. Eilberg-Schwartz suggests that their concern with patrilineal reproduction lies in the nature of the priesthood itself which was passed down from father to son. The priests may have rooted their theology in reproduction in order to increase a people decimated by the Babylonian exile, but there is no doubt that this theology also served to legitimate the priesthood as a kinship of men.

Eilberg-Schwartz perceives tensions that this emphasis on reproduction must have caused within priestly theology. For as Gen. 1.26-28 makes clear, as well as believing that sexuality and reproduction were an essential, created part of being human, the priests also believed that human beings were made in the image of God. What it means to be made in the image of God has always been a matter of contention but very rarely has it even been considered that it might have something to do with bodiliness. Christian theologians have tended to latch on to the tradition that God has no physical form (Deut. 4.12-24). The authors of this Deuteronomic passage advance this as the reason for the ancient prohibition on making images of God. To be made in God's image, therefore, is assumed to be about abstract qualities, not embodiment. Yet such an interpretation of Genesis 1 is not unproblematic:

> On the one hand, human embodiment and sexuality are considered good; but they are good because God said so (Gen. 1.31), and because they are products of God's creative activity. Yet at the same time they are the very symbols of human difference from God… For this reason, there is a tension between obeying God and being like God. A person who wishes to obey God should be fruitful and multiply. But in doing so, one engages precisely that dimension of human experience that denies one's similarity to God. In fact, sexual intercourse contaminates a couple, alienating them from the sacred and hence from God (Eilberg-Schwartz 1997: 45).

Yet, several passages in the Hebrew Scriptures suggest that God did have some bodily form and that it at least resembled that of a human being (Exod. 24.9-11; 33.17, 23; 1 Kgs 22.19; Amos 9.1; Isa. 6.1; Ezek. 1.26-28; Dan. 7.9). Could humanity then image God in terms of embodiment—certainly the Hebrew word translated as 'image' (*tselem*) is used elsewhere, for example in Gen. 5.1-3 to describe a physical likeness or resemblance between people. Some scholars suggest that the addition of the abstract word *demut* or 'likeness' deliberately shifts the emphasis away from the bodily but others have pointed out that the term has some connection with the word for 'blood' and therefore emphasizes physical kinship. Even in this strand, God's body is never fully evident, always at least partly disguised. The reason for this may be to conceal God's sex, thus avoiding questions of how both sexes can image God. God turns his *panai*, which can be translated as 'face' or 'front side', from Moses (Exod. 33.17-33) and Eilberg-Schwartz sees a parallel here with the story of Noah's sons who turn their faces away from their father's nakedness (Gen. 9.20-27). Throughout the Hebrew

Scriptures the dominant images of God do suggest masculinity and this would create enormous problems for ancient Israelite males for Israel is often represented as being the female lover or wife of God (Hos. 1–3; Ezek. 16.23). Since we have already seen that the priests understood Israel primarily as a gathering of males, 'the body of a God who is male thus potentially evokes homoeroticism, that is, erotic love of a human male for a divine father. Homoeroticism is a problem only because it comes into conflict with the dominant image of masculinity in ancient Judaism' (Eilberg-Schwartz 1995: 145)—which as we have seen was constructed by the priests in terms of reproduction. The veiling of God's body thus protects Israel from the fate of Ham who had to be punished for fixing his erotic gaze upon his father. Other problems also arise if God is attributed with a male sex, for the monotheistic male God of the priests does not reproduce and thus human sexual organs are as problematic as if God had no body at all.

Feminist biblical scholar Phyllis Trible argues that in Genesis 1 sexuality (as opposed to reproduction) is what distinguishes human beings from animals who are classified to their kind. The use of female as well as male images of God in the Hebrew Scriptures suggests that it is in their sexuality that men and women image God (Trible 1987). Trible does not consider the possibility of God having a body, yet without a body God's sexuality is at best simply a metaphorical, at worse a meaningless concept. Is God androgynous? Stephen Moore in his post-modernist exploration of the divine body in the Hebrew and Christian Scriptures points out that this was the conclusion some of the rabbis came to, Adam being created with two faces and subsequently sawn in two by his creator (Moore 1996: 90-91). Yet human beings do not tend to be androgynous and so once again our bodies are problematized. Some contemporary theologians have taken something of this idea and developed it into what is known as the theory of complementarity. Men and women are considered to be different and complementary. It is when men and women come together in the act of creation/reproduction that they image God most clearly. This theology is not found in the either the Hebrew Scriptures or the New Testament. In addition, the androgynous God is not found outside the confines of Genesis 1, a handful of female images of God being thoroughly swamped by a preponderance of male imagery.

Eilberg-Schwartz wants to suggest that the tensions and confusion in and caused by Gen. 1.26-28 are deliberate and are compounded by the

use of both the singular and the plural in references to God and humanity. The point is to mask the tensions. He points out that these tensions
are not shared by other ancient Israelite writers but are the specific result
of the priestly insistence that human beings are not fundamentally different from God but made in the image of God. If there is a huge ontological gap between human beings and God then human beings would of
course have needs and behaviours which God did not—the body is not
a problem. But in priestly theology,

> the human body is caught between contending cultural impulses...
> While the priests regard reproduction as one of the most important reli-
> gious injunctions, semen is contaminating, even if ejaculated during a
> legitimate act of intercourse (Lev. 15.16-18)... In the very act of carrying
> out God's will, one alienated oneself from God by becoming contami-
> nated (Eilberg-Schwartz 1997: 52).

A human being is made in God's image: God does not reproduce but
God commands human reproduction. For the priest the human body
was pulled in two different directions. Eilberg-Schwartz suggests that
obsession with the intimate control of the body actually served to divert
attention from the wider more problematic issues, but as an object of
obsession the body became symbolic of a number of theological ideas
and themes, such as the covenant, procreation, descent, life and death.

Bodies were not unproblematic in ancient Israel. The desire of the
priestly school to control the body was taken up subsequently by groups
within Judaism such as the Qumran community and the rabbis.

Turning now to the Christian Scriptures or New Testament, many
different views emerge of Jesus' attitude to bodies. William Countryman
(1989) argues that what was distinctly radical about Jesus was his refusal
to acknowledge the two concepts his ancestors in faith had used to
interpret and control the body—purity (Mk 7.18-23) and property (for
example, the concept of male ownership of women's bodies).

Stephen Moore believes that the hypermasculine God of the Hebrew
Scriptures is incarnated in the person of Jesus and that the Gospels can
be read as a bodybuilding manual, with Jesus constantly at work, prepar-
ing his own body to do the impossible—defeat the destruction of death
(Moore 1996: 102-17). On the other hand disabled theologians have
reminded us that at the moment when Christians perceive who Jesus
really is, that is, at his resurrection, he is revealed as the disabled God,
bearing the marks of rejection and injustice (Eiesland 1994: 89-105).

What are we to make of Jesus' teaching in Mk 12.18-50 on the lack

58INTRODUCING BODY THEOLOGY

of marriage in heaven because people are 'like angels'? Some have suggested that Jesus was disassociating himself from contemporary Jewish apocalypticism, which envisaged a forthcoming millennium in which the dead would be resurrected and married, and that by denying the ultimate enduring of marriage and therefore reproduction Jesus was reflecting belief in an asexual, disembodied future existence. Such an interpretation assumes that Jews at the time regarded angels as sexless, disembodied creatures, which was not the case. It is possible, then, to interpret this piece of teaching as a broadside against the interpretation and legitimization of the body in terms of marriage and reproduction and therefore as evidence of Jesus' liberation of all bodies from the primary institutions of control and ordering.

It is also possible to read the construction of Jesus' body in the Gospels as a site of profound and subversive hospitality. Bruce Malina (1996: 228-35) has pointed out that hospitality meant something quite different in the ancient Mediterranean world to what it means in postmodern western culture. It was not about entertaining family or friends or business contacts, it was about the transformation of the outsider, the stranger, into the guest. This procedure was imperative in societies which viewed the world in terms of insiders and outsiders, as most ancient societies did.

In that world dependence upon the kindness and hospitality of strangers was often the only means for survival. The 'stranger' was often not another who had to be loved but yourself in need of food, shelter and clothing (Deut. 10.18). The *gerîm* (resident aliens), along with others who were economically vulnerable—the poor, widows and orphans—were recognized to be in the position that Israel was in Egypt and therefore deserving of hospitality and inclusion in Israelite life. The story of Sodom (Gen. 19) tells of the evil of inhospitality, of fear and rejection of the stranger. How ironic then that within the Christian tradition the story of the destruction of Sodom for its cruelty towards two male strangers who take shelter in Lot's home should have been twisted into a 'text of terror' and used against gay and lesbian people, itself becoming an instrument of inhospitality.

Julia Kristeva (1982: 90-112) suggests that behind the Levitical laws of the holiness code was a desire to separate the people of Israel from the cult of the mother goddesses to which they stubbornly clung (Jer. 7.18; 44.17). Menstrual blood and birth blood, two powerful symbols of bodily hospitality, are made into taboos. Certainly yearnings for a hospitable theology express themselves, particularly in the writings of Second and Third Isaiah where a different reaction to the pain of exile is occasionally mirrored in maternal imagery applied to Yahweh and to Zion (Isa. 48.15-15; 50.1; 66.7-9) and in imagery of a new creation which has hospitality at its heart (Isa. 60.11; Isa. 56.3-8). Kristeva maintains that Jesus' theoretical and practical abolition of the purity laws (Mk 7.1-23) indicates that he managed to achieve within his own being a reconciliation between the maternal and the linguistic (law) orders. In Mark's narrative the abolition of the purity laws is followed by the story of the Syrophoenician woman (7.24-30). This structuring of the narrative is significant: after making a full-scale attack on the purity system Jesus has his theory tested by a Gentile woman. His reaction is shameful. But this woman, the fiercely protective mother, demands the hospitality that he has declared to be possible (albeit implicitly). '[B]e prepared for the coming of the Stranger, Be prepared for him who knows how to ask questions' warns T.S. Eliot in *Choruses from 'The Rock'* (Eliot 1963: 171). The Syrophoenician woman is the stranger who knows how to ask questions about Jesus' own praxis and in the process changes him, making him more hospitable.

Jesus' life begins in an extraordinary act of maternal hospitality, the receiving of a stranger whose presence brought danger and potential destruction (Lk. 1.26-56). That which Leviticus had declared unclean becomes the site of incarnation and the body of Israel which brings to birth its messiah is not the taut, clearly defined, closed ideal body of some parts of Leviticus but the generous, expansive, accommodating, open, exuding body of Mary, which needs generous flesh to shelter, nourish and nurture its stranger/guest. If the purity laws were at least to some extent about the abolition of the maternal, with one consequence being the making of Israel (at least to the extent that it was influenced by priestly ideology) into an inhospitable body, Mary in co-operation with others reverses that.

Mary's son spends his life incarnating hospitality. In the Gospels Jesus is portrayed most often and most obviously in the role of stranger/guest, never, with the possible exception of the Zacchaeus story (Lk. 19.1-10), imposing himself on a host or taking over the role of the host. Jesus and his followers appear to have lived an itinerant lifestyle, making them rely upon the hospitality of others. Luke notes that they were particularly dependent upon the hospitality of a group of women who travelled with them (8.1-3). The Jesus body (Jesus and his followers) was then deeply vulnerable because it constructed itself as a permanent stranger in a world (Jewish and Gentile) where to be a stranger was to be at risk of social or physical rejection. The gospels seem to suggest that Jesus constructed his community in opposition to the crucial family unit which was the foundation of his society and through which the outsider/insider classifications were defined and maintained (Mk 3.31-35; Mt. 10.35-37) (Malina 1996: 35-66). In other words, Jesus incarnated his ministry outside of, and therefore against, the social system which created 'strangers', by becoming a stranger himself. Jesus' vulnerability as a stranger is emphasized in his periodic rejection by 'his own', which reaches its climax in the crucifixion. In the account of Simon the Pharisee's treatment of Jesus (Lk. 7.36-50), the woman who was a 'sinner' offers the hospitality to Jesus' body that Simon has withheld. Immediately before this story Luke reports the accusation made against Jesus, 'look a glutton and drunkard, a friend of tax-collectors and sinners' (Lk. 7.34). E.P. Sanders is convinced that these sayings give us access to the scandal of Jesus, because even though Luke links the hospitality Jesus received from 'sinners' (i.e. people who lived totally outside of the law, better referred to as the 'wicked' according to Sanders) to their repentance, the other gospels do not. If Jesus had only accepted hospitality from these people on condition of their repentance or in order to precipitate their repentance, his actions would not have caused any scandal. The scandal can only be explained by the fact that 'he ate and drank with the wicked and told them that God especially loved them, and that the kingdom was at hand' (Sanders 1993: 223). By accepting the hospitality of the wicked Jesus in his own body preaches the way that Yahweh operates to save, to bring in his reign, namely through inclusion rather than exclusion, through extravagant, reckless generosity in which all debts are cancelled. The reign of God is a warm, fleshy, all-encompassing body with enough spare flesh for all to be nourished. This is enacted with particular subtlety by Jesus for he does not offer hospitality to the wicked: the stranger is always dependent upon the host and therefore always in position of gratitude and disempowerment. No, Jesus makes himself dependent upon the hospitality of the wicked, thus emphasizing their empowerment in the reign of God. They are not let in by the skin of their teeth, they are not included because of some special dispensation after everyone else, in fact they are entering the kingdom before everyone else (Mt. 21.22). None of this makes any sense within the social system in which Jesus had to operate but that was the point, the kingdom was to overturn all of that. No wonder those who had the authority and responsibility for maintaining the clear lines of the body, for policing the crucial insider/outsider parameters, should find Jesus' behaviour scandalous. They, of course, would have believed in the honourable principle of hospitality but within clear boundaries. Jesus trespasses over those boundaries. One of the apparently unusual aspects of Jesus' ministry was not that he used the metaphor of the banquet to describe the future kingdom (Mt. 22.1-14; Lk. 14.15-24), which was not common, but not unique, but that he seems to have regarded the meals he ate as symbolic of that future banquet (Sanders 1993: 185-87). The Jesus of the Gospels is an eating, drinking, touching, expansive figure, the Jesus of Stanley Spencer rather than the anorexic figure of Victorian piety or Moore's taut bodybuilder.

There is, of course, one point in the Gospels where Jesus becomes host rather than guest and that is the night when he is arrested. Here he returns the hospitality he has received throughout his public ministry in one suitably exaggerated and sensual gesture. The host becomes the hospitality, the food and drink on which his guests can survive until the kingdom comes. Jesus' last symbolic act is one of outrageous self-giving and therefore vulnerability—a fact which is rammed home to us as the gospel writers then unfold exactly what is done with his body. The one who offers perpetual hospitality to all willing to sit at the table ends up as the stranger destroyed on the cross. But the cold, stark, mean world of death cannot contain the body of Jesus; it is too warm, too big, too generous. He rises to give and receive hospitality again, to eat and drink and enjoy friendship and to provide a perpetual, eternal source of nourishment to those to whom he gives his spirit and who become his body on earth (Jn 20.19-23).

Jesus' death is not the climax of a 'no pain, no gain' theology, but the punishment inflicted on a stranger who cannot be conformed to the laws of the society in which he sought a home, in this case his own society. His resurrection is the divine vindication of hospitality over meanness and inclusion over exclusion. The resurrection returns us to the place where the gospel began. Through a young woman's labour, pain and blood an all-encompassing hospitality was brought to birth in her world and through the labour, pain and blood of her son on a cross that hospitality was made universal. The young woman in labour and the man on the cross are part of the same process of salvation and that process goes on, the process of bringing to birth a new way of being, a new creation based upon mutual hospitality, symbolized in Revelation by the woman giving birth to the child of the new creation (Rev. 12).

In the letters of Paul we find a complex approach to the body. Paul was not a dualist: nowhere in his letters do we find a contrast between body (*soma*) and soul or spirit (*psyche*). There is a persistent contrast between flesh (*sarx*) and spirit (*pneuma*) which we must not read in terms of a body/soul dualism. Paul uses the term 'flesh' as a kind of shorthand to describe the human being (body and soul) in its fallen state and 'spirit' to describe the person in its redeemed state (Gal. 5.17). Paul's theology is thoroughly embodied:

> It is from the body of sin and death that we are delivered; it is through the body of Christ on the Cross that we are saved; it is into the body of the Church that we are incorporated; it is by his body in the Eucharist that the Community is sustained; it is in our body that its new life has to be manifest; it is to a resurrection of this body to the likeness of his glorious body that we are destined (Robinson 1952: 9).

The *soma* of the eucharist connects the *soma* of the believers with the corporate *soma* of the Church which is the *soma* of Christ. Yet, for Paul the body, while called to be the temple of the Spirit and site of the glorification of God (1 Cor. 6.9-20), is in need of redemption, weakened by sin and liable to sin. This redemption is achieved through the cross.

Stephen Moore has noted that in the Pauline corpus the cross is above all else a place of sacrificial blood, of torture and of the power of divine wrath, a place of public punishment. In Paul's theology punishment and reform are held together. The believer has to bear the same punishment as and with Christ but through that punishment begins the process of transformation and reform. The Christian body becomes the centre of that transformation. The indwelling spirit of God is a down payment, a guarantee of the future inheritance (2 Cor. 1.22; 5.5) (Moore 1996: 11-34).

The impact of redemption upon the body is for Paul above all else to transfer it from one form of slavery to another. The body is essentially enslaved, either to sin or to Christ: having been 'bought with a price' (1 Cor. 6.20) by Christ's death and resurrection, it is obliged to live a life of complete self-giving which mirrors that of Christ's. The implications of this enslavement are most clearly evident in Paul's teaching on marriage. Husbands and wives are instructed to hand authority over their bodies to each other (1 Cor. 7.3-4). Here enslavement could be read to guarantee radical mutual equality between male and female bodies but elsewhere in the Pauline corpus it becomes clear that all may be slaves but some are more enslaved than others. In Eph. 5.22-33 wives are instructed to be subject or obedient (*hypotassethai*) to their husbands, 'for the husband is the head of the wife just as Christ is the head of the church', just as children and slaves are later instructed to be subject or obedient (*hypotassethai*) to their parents and masters whereas the husband is instructed to 'love' his wife because she is part of his body—part of his property in other words. This construction of married bodies is also found in Col. 3.18-22. The language of slavery is always going to be problematic for women and indeed for all who find themselves in relationships in which one party is structured as an inferior to another by wider society. Even if we were to accept that Paul's language of mutual authority meant to bespeak radical equality between men and women, such radical equality would first have to be realized outside the bedroom before it could be celebrated within it. Only people with equal power could hand that power over to another in a way that enacted and achieved radical mutuality, in which case the language of slavery would be redundant because slavery is about radical inequality and debt.[2] This language also grates against the language of the Gospels which portray Jesus as the one who seeks to instigate a new order in which all debt, and therefore debt slavery, is wiped out. Peter Selby is convinced that the elevation of debt and indebtedness to theological categories has actually prevented the Church from confronting the evil of economic debt and its death-dealing effect upon the bodies of men and women and children throughout the world (Selby 1997: 156-68).

For Paul, then, embodiment is an essential part of being human and the body is intimately involved in the process of redemption, in the process of undergoing transformation. The final transformation is participation in the resurrection of Christ, during which the body will undergo a change similar to a seed as it germinates (1 Cor. 15.35-55), continuity in change. What believers did with their bodies was therefore an intrinsic part of Christian witness for Paul and one of the most obvious means of distinguishing followers of Christ from others. At times Paul's body theology led him to diverge radically from his inherited tradition, for example, when he disrupts the ordering of men and women's bodies into reproduction and recommends celibacy (1 Cor. 7.32-34) or

2.   For a full theological analysis of debt and debt slavery in the ancient and modern worlds see Selby 1997.

clearly proclaims the equality of all bodies (Gal. 3.28) but at other times
he reproduces the gender hierarchies and social-symbolic ordering of
the bodies found in the priestly writings. This is evident, for example, in
his treatment of same-sex desire in Rom. 1.26-27. He assumes that all
are aware of a natural sexual order (which he himself sets out in 1 Cor.
11.1-16 using the bodily image of the 'head' to state that the natural
order of creation is for woman to be subordinate to man, and a fulfiller
of his needs) but some have rejected it and given themselves up to the
unnatural use of sexual organs. For Paul, as for his priestly ancestors and
Jewish contemporaries, 'natural' intercourse was vaginal intercourse
between men and women and it was natural precisely because it
symbolically enacted the social hierarchy of men and women. Same-sex
sexual intercourse disrupted this divinely sanctioned order.[3] Paul's body
theology veers between the radical and the conservative (within a matter
of verses the body can be employed both as a metaphor of radical
authority and rigid hierarchy—1 Cor. 12.12-31) as he attempts to work
out the implications of salvation on the hoof and in response to real
people and situations. The body, however, is always central.

Change and Decay: The Body and Early Christianity

As Christianity spread into the Roman Empire it found itself working
against a philosophical background which was dualistic in nature. The
Hellenistic philosophies it encountered did not preach or practise hatred
of the body but saw the body as fundamentally different from the soul
and prone to change, decay, disease and destabilization of the self (all of
which were regarded as being the antithesis of perfection and divinity).
Until the soul could unshackle itself from this burdensome matter,
which tended to drag it away from the One, and return to that One, the
body had to be controlled and policed through the practice of asceti-
cism—a term originally applied to the training of athletes was now
applied to the gentle training of the body. As we have already seen,
there was enough anxiety over the body in the Judaeo-Christian tradition for such philosophy to 'speak' to early Christianity. Yet belief in
the resurrection meant that the early Christians could never long for
complete disembodiment and this served to prevent most from falling
into a dualistic attitude to the human person. Caroline Walker Bynum

---

3.   For a full discussion of Paul's attitude to same-sex relationships, particularly
as they relate to women see Brooten 1996: 189-303.

has demonstrated that obsession with the nature of the resurrected body in early Christianity expresses both a disgust with bodily decay and a conviction that a person could not be a person without a body (Bynum 1995). The earthly body had to be rid of its tendency to change and decay but its identity had to be preserved. In part this continuity was considered necessary in order to ensure that, in the resurrected life, gender hierarchy remained in place.

Attitudes to the body in the early Church were not uniform. The *Didascalia of Apostles*, a Syrian work of the fourth century based upon a third-century Greek text, proclaimed that because Christ assumed a body and raised that body from death nothing can make the body impure, not even menstrual or birth blood or semen or the decay of death.[4] This was a far cry from the teaching of some of the Christian Gnostics, such as the second-century Valentinus for whom matter and the body had nothing to do with God but resulted from rebelliousness against him. Matter encased the spirit which did belong to the true God. It was this spirit that Christ came to liberate from the shackles of matter, including gender differentiation. Between these two extremes stood most Christian theologians, rejecting the Gnostic view that matter is evil and does not belong to God but, like Paul, aware that the body was prone to decay and in need of redemption. The ascetic movement within Christianity became the means through which believers could incarnate the resurrected body within society and thus signal the forthcoming collapse of that society. In particular by renouncing marriage and childbirth Christians differentiated themselves from society around them and symbolically threatened the perpetuation of that society. The young virgin body became the most powerful symbol of the transformed resurrected body (Brown 1988). Some eastern Christian writers bought into the notion also found in the Jewish philosopher Philo that there had been two creations, the first of pure spiritual beings who turned away from God and fell, with God then in a second creation providing them with bodies. Origen was the most fervent Christian advocate of the double creation but it is also found in a number of eastern theologians such as Gregory of Nyssa and Maximus the Confessor. Whilst they were careful not to associate the second creation of bodies with evil, they were clear that it was a lesser good marked by body/soul and gender duality. For advocates of this position, redemption involved an ultimate return to a pre-fallen and therefore a genderless state, by

4.   *Didascalia Apostolorum*, ch. 26.

which most writers seem to have meant a male state, women's bodies being particularly associated with change and decay (Louth 1997: 114-16). Once again the virgin or celibate is one who incarnates the process of salvation having left the second creation and is in the process of returning to the first.

Still, even when theologians saw redemption as involving redemption from the earthly body, they found it hard to conceive of existence without bodiliness. In the west Ambrose of Milan (c. 339–97) was as concerned as were the Levitical priests of old with boundaries and in particular the boundary between the Catholic Church and the world which threatened to 'pollute' it and render it soft and effeminate.

> He viewed the body as a perilous mudslick, on which the firm tread of the soul's resolve might slip and tumble at any moment. He had seen courtiers suffer the ultimate indignity of falling topsy-turvy as they hustled along the smooth corridors of the Imperial palace. The world *lubricum*, 'slippery', carried an exceptionally heavy charge of negative meaning for him: it signified moments of utter helplessness, of frustration, of fatal loss of inner balance and of surrender to the instincts brought about by the tragic frailty of the physical body (Brown 1988: 349).

This slipperiness was particularly evident in the scar of sexuality, the result of the fall. Redemption therefore involved liberation from this slippery flesh but not liberation from all flesh, for Ambrose believed that virgin birth signalled God's intention to provide a new flesh, devoid of this terrible scar, the body of Christ into which Christians were baptized. He therefore believed that the Christian life should be one of sexual continence manifesting this new flesh.[5]

Ambrose's disciple, Augustine of Hippo (354–430), abandoned the idea of a double creation, finding it irreconcilable with the biblical account of creation. Human beings were created embodied, gendered and sexual. Adam and Eve must have enjoyed sexual relations in the garden of Eden, their desire for each other being completely under the control of their wills. This rationality, however, was tragically disrupted at the fall, when concupiscence, the overpowering desire for material or sensual gratification, overwhelmed the human will once and for all. The human body becomes in Augustine a battle ground between the will and concupiscence, between reason and humanity's animal nature, and the battle was focused for Augustine in a particularly obvious way in the male genitals:

5.   Ambrose, *Expositio in Evangelium Secundum Lucam* 5.24.

> When it comes to children being generated, the members created for this purpose do not obey the will, but lust has to be waited for to set these members in motion, as having rights over them, and sometimes it will not act when the mind is willing, while sometimes it even acts against the mind's will![6]

For Augustine human beings are simply overpowered by lust, which drags their minds away from God. To desire such a state is to desire evil, for it is to desire the privation of good, the loss of what human beings ought to be, rational and in control of their bodies. Therefore the most effective way to realign our wills with God's was to practise celibacy. Sexual activity could be justified as reproduction but even then was not entirely sinless.

Generally speaking, the Eastern Church took a more positive attitude to body and sexuality than the Western Church—not banning married men from the priesthood unlike the West eventually did. Clement of Alexandria (c. 150–c. 215), even though he adopted the stoic belief that human beings are disturbed and disordered by passions and desires and that the ideal is the passionless state of *apatheia*, described the body as the 'soul's consort and ally', essential to redemption, and located the image of God in human beings' ability to procreate (Ware 1997: 97). Married couples should undertake sexual activity consciously, motivated by the desire to procreate rather than by unconscious, pleasure-seeking passion. Control of the body was also to be exercised outside of the bedroom: Christians must belch, sit and eat with decorum. It was as an embodied person that a Christian stood before God. This perception of the body as friend *and* enemy was to echo down the Christian ages.

From its earliest days then the Church exhibited an ambivalent attitude to the body captured succinctly by the seventh-century eastern theologian John Climacus, 'He is my helper and my enemy, my assistant and my opponent, a protector and a traitor' (Ware 1997: 90).

Body Knowledge in the Middle Ages

The ambiguous attitude to the body demonstrated by the early Church theologians persists in the mediaeval period. The dominating figure of this period is Thomas Aquinas (c. 1225–74) whose use of Aristotelian philosophy to provide a *Summa Theologiae* (an inquiry into Christian theology for those beginning religious life) led him to assert the unity of

6.   Augustine, *De Nuptiis et Concupiscentia* 1.6.

the body and soul: the soul being the substantial form or pattern of the human body, that part of human nature which is everlasting and which orders the material. The soul/intellect needs the bodily senses in order to abstract knowledge but it is the soul/intellect which is spiritual and it alone images God. The soul can exist without the body and, even though it is imperfect in such a state, it does not desire the body.[7]

Continued suspicion of the body accompanied an increasing emphasis upon the sacraments, relics, the sufferings of Christ and the idealization of courtly love. The increasing emphasis upon the sacraments accompanied an increased clericalism which resulted in the gradual exclusion of women from ecclesiastical power. One of the consequences of this was a deeply embodied form of female mysticism. Visions gave women authority and a voice in the Church at a time when they were losing both. They also enabled women to bypass the increasingly masculinized structures of the Church. Gertrude (1256–c. 1302), for example, was assured by Christ in a vision that he would 'enter' her and 'renew in your soul all the seven sacraments in one operation more efficaciously than any other priest or pontiff can do by seven separate acts' (Bynum 1982: 202). What is extraordinary is the deeply embodied, erotic nature of many of these encounters between women and Christ. Male theologians employed erotic images for the purpose of allegorizing the soul's relationship to God,

> With the women there is a direct, highly charged, passionate encounter between Christ and the writer. The sexuality is explicit, and there is no warning that it should not be taken literally. There is no intellectualising or spiritualising, no climbing up into the head, or using the erotic as an allegory hedged about with warnings. To be sure, the sexual encounter is also a spiritual one; moral and spiritual lessons are to be learned. But they are to be learned, not by allegorising what is happening, but by highly charged encounter (Jantzen 1995: 133).

Such encounters with Christ often left their physical marks in the form of stigmata on the bodies of these women. It also informed their theology. In the writings of the English mystic Julian of Norwich (c. 1342–c. 1416) we encounter a woman concerned to see the reintegration of our 'sensuality' and our 'substance'. Our substance is always united with God but our sensuousness, which includes our bodiliness and consciousness, is alienated from him. The road to salvation involves not the ditching of our sensuality but the reintegration of our two

7.   Aquinas, *Sup.*, q. 93, art 1.

natures, just as Christ unified his two natures in one person. Julian, then, had no interest in demonizing sexuality or the body (Jantzen 1995: 146-56).

One of the more difficult aspects of mediaeval women's spirituality for our contemporary minds to grasp was their self-imposed excessive fasting. Various explanations have been offered for this phenomenon. Piero Camporesi suggests that it has something to do with the increasing emphasis on the eucharist, coupled with the continuing ambiguity towards the human body. The thought of the body of Christ journeying down through the human body into the bowels caused some anxiety and hence it was necessary, particularly for that gender more closely associated with the flesh, to ensure that the body was appropriately purified before the body of Christ entered (Camporesi 1987: 1.221-37). Rudolph Bell (1985) associates a desire to control the body with a desire by women to resist male control. Caroline Walker Bynum, on the other hand, argues that fasting had such a central place in women's spirituality in the Middle Ages because it was food (rather than wealth or world power) that women had control over and it was the giving up of what one had control over that led to holiness (Bynum 1987).

There is still deep ambiguity towards the body, particularly the female body, in most of the writings of mediaeval women mystics, but we can observe how these women subverted the patriarchal association of fleshiness with femaleness by obtaining bodily knowledge of Christ in their own flesh. This gave them an authority which men in the Church struggled to control.

To Dance or Not to Dance: The Body and the Reformation

It would be easy to sketch the Reformation as a retreat from bodiliness to inwardness, associated as it is with the reform and spiritualizing of the sacramental system and the priority of the Word, justification by faith alone and private judgment, but this would be a caricature. Martin Luther, as well as retaining a strong belief in the real presence of Christ in the eucharist and a thoroughly corporate image of the Church, also maintained a Pauline distinction between the flesh and spirit which meant that the body, just as much as the soul, had to be redeemed. He imagined heaven to be a place of dancing and refused to condemn this practice which many of his contemporaries perceived as particularly immoral (Tripp 1997: 134-37). Ulrich Zwingli's denial of the real presence of Christ in the eucharist was not in any sense a reaction against embodiment. On the contrary, his denial stemmed from his belief that the body and blood of Christ had risen to heaven at the resurrection and therefore could not be present on earth as well. Zwingli was convinced of the value of the human body in the sight of God and perhaps more than any other of the major Reformers emphasized the Church's nature as the body of Christ (Tripp 1997: 137-38). It is in the writings of John Calvin that a rather more pessimistic attitude to the body is found. He found it hard to believe that the image of God in humanity extends to the body but accepted that it must. His emphasis was on inward disposition, the mystical rather than the real presence of Christ in the Eucharist, and he regarded dancing as the prologue to immorality (Tripp 1997: 138-41).

Of course, one of the most radical aspects of the Protestant Reformation was the de-idealizing of virginity. Not only did the Reformers find no scriptural warrant for the superiority of the celibate state, they also believed that compulsory celibacy led to immorality among priests and religious. Marriage prevented such fornication. Yet we must be careful about interpreting the rehabilitation of marriage as an entirely positive phenomenon. Certainly for many women the Protestant Reformation signalled a narrowing of their bodily choices. A concerted propaganda campaign against the nun, explicitly associating her with prostitution, coupled with the dissolution of the monasteries, meant that women were totally collapsed into the roles of wife and mother with no other choices before them. Nor did the idealizing of marriage dispel Christian ambivalence towards the body and sexual desire. Daniel Doriani has charted the complex attitudes of the Puritans to marriage (Doriani 1996: 33-51). Puritans regarded wedlock as an honourable and chaste state and went beyond other Protestants like Luther in regarding sexual activity as an act essential to marriage—not simply because it prevented fornication and resulted in procreation, but because it increased the love between men and women who had an equal right to be satisfied. Nevertheless they feared excessive desire, on the grounds that it reduced human beings to the level of animals. As a result the bodies of married couples had to be disciplined. Spontaneity was curtailed by the requirement that couples pray before intercourse. Levitical laws on the timing of sexual intercourse were to be observed. Couples who failed to practise moderation would be punished by the birth of deformed children. This fear of excess was not confined to sex but also applied to eating, drinking and recreation. Doriani attributes this ambiguity to the fact that the Puritans 'strove to restore pure scriptural teaching to England but could not break free from their cultural and intellectual bonds' (Doriani 1996: 49) which emphasized the dangers of excess and the value of moderation in all things.

The Enlightenment and Beyond

It was Rene Descartes (1596–1650) who ushered in the era of profound body/soul dualism, arguing that the mind is a substance completely distinct from the body. Thereafter human reason became the sole key to unlocking the external world, with nature becoming a vast soulless plane of matter to be examined, ordered and classified by the human mind. Stephen Moore has noted that in the age of Enlightenment two sacred bodies were suddenly open to scrutiny and analysis, the human body at the hand of the anatomist and the body of Scripture at the hands of biblical critics. Dissection of both by human reason, in order to classify and understand and control, became acceptable (Moore 1996: 37-72). The age of the Enlightenment as well as establishing a radical distinction between body and soul also declared a radical distinction between male and female bodies. Up to this point western culture, influenced by ancient authorities such as Galen and Aristotle, had maintained that men and women shared the same basic anatomy. Women's bodies differed from men only to the extent that their genital organs were internal. Male and female organs were not linguistically distinguished. Female bodies were regarded as being inferior to men's, but though there were two genders there was basically only one sex (Laqueur 1990). Gender was often viewed as unstable and changeable, a view that we can also find reflected to some extent in the writing of St Paul who, while appearing to advocate a rigid hierarchical distinction between male and female, actually renders gender theologically slippery, as even Karl Barth was forced to recognize. The image of the Church as Christ's bride renders all within it—including men—female and the call for all members of the Church to act as Christ to others implicitly urges women to perform 'male' roles (Loughlin 1998). Such is our modern preoccupation with fixed gender and sexual identities that we can fail to wrestle with the subtleties of the premodern understanding of sex as exhibited, for example, in Paul's letters. Thomas Laqueur argues that the eighteenth-century change in the understanding of human sexuality had little to do with the advance of science (after all the clitoris had been 'discovered' by men a couple of centuries before with no change in the understanding of the human body) and more to do with politics: 'There were endless new struggles for power and position in the enormously enlarged public sphere of the eighteenth and particularly post nineteenth centuries: between and among men and women; between and among feminists and antifeminists' (Laqueur 1990: 152).

Ironically, the eclipse of the body by reason that took place during the Enlightenment enabled women to claim authority on the basis of reason. The emphasis on the individual as a moral agent enabled women to claim moral autonomy. Disembodied objectivity held out the promise of liberation for women. One response to this was the development of a two-sex model. Gender, if it was going to continue to serve the power of men, had to be regrounded and it was relocated in a radical distinction between female and male bodies. Male and female sexual organs were linguistically distinguished. The differences between male and female bodies were read to reflect fundamental, ontological differences between men and women which took women out of the public sphere (Hitchcock 1996).

Many theologians of all denominations in the modern period capitulated to this dualism, with the body ceasing to have any ultimate value or purpose in redemption. Paul Tillich, one of the giants of liberal theology, in his construction of Being located it in the internal, individual self. The *angst* and alienation from which humanity was saved through New Being was not located in a material, embodied world but in the human psyche. Thus all, however rich or poor, oppressed or free, were assumed to be suffering from the same *angst* and open to the same subjective transformation through the grasp of New Being. The body was vaporized and with it divine acknowledgment and concern for those whose bodies are not free (Tillich 1951–63). Exceptions to this trend included Karl Barth, who read enormous theological significance into male and female biological difference, regarding it as a reflection and symbol of the relationship of God to Israel, Christ to the Church, and I to Thou (Barth 1960: III, 2, 286-314) and the French Roman Catholic theologian Pierre Teilhard de Chardin, who embraced the scientific theory of evolution and concluded that the whole universe was in a process of evolution heading towards a supreme state of consciousness, called the omega-point, of which Christ is the incarnation. All things including matter are being drawn towards perfection in God (Teilhard 1959 and 1960).

Ambiguity Continues

A partial sweep through the Christian tradition thus reveals that thoroughgoing dualism is an extremely recent phenomenon. It was never universally adhered to and now is generally rejected under the influence of various theologies of liberation. Much more characteristic of the Christian tradition is an uneasy acceptance of embodiment: uneasy because the body is liable to decay, excess, instability and distraction, whereas perfection is associated with changeless stability. Nevertheless there is generally a clear sense that the body and soul are in the process of redemption together.

This ambiguity towards the body exists among Christians in an age when the importance of the body and the dangers of dualism are accepted by even the most conservative theologians. Pope John Paul II is a good example of a deeply conservative theologian who has wrestled with the meaning of the body. To understand Pope John Paul's attitude to the body is to understand his attitude to homosexuality, marriage and contraception. He has a 'high' view of the body, recognizing that 'it is on the basis of the body and not simply self-awareness and self-determination that one is a "subject"'' (John Paul II 1981: 109). From the two creation accounts in Genesis the Pope concludes that the original divinely willed meaning of the body is 'nuptial', by which he means that the body is meant for union, for the giving and receiving of persons as gift, for community. Of course, the Pope does not confine such union to heterosexual marriage—all are called to make a gift of themselves for the sake of the kingdom, but how this is done will differ according to vocation—but his theology of the body does lead him to centralize sexuality in the human person. It is not simply a matter of biology or animal nature. Human bodies should never be objectified or used simply for personal gratification for they are created for mutual, self-giving relationship and in this respect they image the nature of their creator.

So far there would be little to separate the Pope's understanding of the body from that of most theologians of liberation, but the Pope shares with most of his ancestors in faith a deep distrust of bodily desire which he too identifies with concupiscence. It is this concupiscence, the cause and result of the fall, which has led to the obscuring of the nuptial meaning of the body. Human beings are thus disposed to treat others simply as objects for self-gratification. This violates both the nuptial meaning of the body and nature. Following Aquinas the Pope maintains that the divine will revealed in natural law is that sexual activity should lead to procreation. To engage in sexual activity which cannot lead to procreation is to engage in sexual activity purely for the purposes of enjoyment which is concupiscence and therefore sinful. For the Pope there is a huge distinction between love and desire. Love is a virtue, an acquired disposition to moral good; it is not an emotion but a duty to value a person in accordance with God's will. Love redeems sexual desire by conforming it to natural law. This is why the Pope has staunchly opposed the use of artificial contraception and acceptance of same-sex relationships: in this understanding both forms of sexual activity annul the nuptial meaning of the body, violate the laws of nature and therefore spring from sinful bodily desire. Homosexuality is an 'objective disorder': it must be the result of sin, for God's creation is ordered towards nuptial self-giving which results in procreation. The lesbian or gay person then is called to a form of self-giving which involves, in the words of St Paul, the crucifixion of 'all self indulgent passions and desires', only thus will they be able to affirm the nuptial meaning of the body in their own persons (Congregation for the Doctrine of Faith 1986: para. 12).

Pope John Paul II also uses the theory of complementarity to connect together the nuptial meaning of the body and the rooting of sexual activity in natural law and also draws on the theory of complementarity to justify his 'equal but different' approach to men and women. Physically, psychologically and ontologically women differ from men and 'it is only through the duality of the "masculine" and the "feminine" that the "human" finds full realisation' (John Paul II 1995: 12).

For Pope John Paul, then, the body is essential to personhood and to our purpose of imaging God in self-donation. It has a created meaning, and even a language, which means that using it for purposes other than that willed by the creator is to lie (John Paul II 1980: para. 11; but see Moore 1992: 92-108). The body is also perceived in terms of enemy-hood. Its desires, lust, alienates us from the created order, reduces us to entirely self-centred creatures and makes it hard for us to attain the virtue of love. The Pope therefore exhibits the same deep ambiguity towards the body that we have traced throughout Christian history. It is important to grasp that it is ambiguity, rather than through-going dualism, that characterizes this tradition. A religion which focuses on incarnation and resurrection should always be pulled back from the brink of dualism.

Christian tradition constantly leads us back to the body and warns us against all tendencies to construct the human person and society in terms of disembodied minds. The approach taken by Tillich has been echoed in some types of modern feminism which have reduced gender to a matter of socially constructed behaviour imposed onto a passive body. Liberation involves changing *minds* and the body is vaporized as an instrument of change and site of knowledge. Although this approach was developed to counteract the biological essentialism which so often underlies the theology of complementarity—men and women being different, psychologically and ontologically, because of their different bodies—the body has sometimes been thrown out with the bath water. For the Christian tradition also teaches us that the ambiguity in which the body is held has a great deal to do with the suspicion of female bodiliness and a complex, dialectical association of female bodiliness with imperfection and therefore with anti-divinity. French feminism has drawn out this construction of women's body as 'lack' or 'absence' and insists that it is time for the female body to learn to speak about itself in a place beyond patriarchal language. Tina Beattie has demonstrated that French feminism, particularly in the form of Luce Irigaray, shares with Pope John Paul II both an understanding of the body as a site of divine revelation, a profound appreciation of the embodied differences between men and women, and a conviction that women's liberation lies not in minimizing those differences but discovering them as gift (Beattie 1997: 160-83). They part company over the nature of the essence of woman. Irigaray maintains that western cultural understandings of sexuality are dominantly 'hom(m)osexual' by which she means that they reflect the experience and perspective of men alone. Women are not allowed to be different, only to be shadows and adjuncts of men. Many who wish to ground their theologies of the body and much more beside in sexual differences between men and women betray a purely male understanding of femaleness (Ward 1998). While the Pope believes that essential femaleness has to be 'recovered' and that it is grounded in maternity (a maternity, whether physical or spiritual, which the Pope understands primarily in terms of self-giving to a man, whether husband or saviour), Irigaray is insistent that all understandings of femininity that have been constructed under patriarchy reflect male and not female subjectivity. Women have to discover their own voice and engage in their own reflection upon their experience of embodied difference (Irigaray 1996). The result of such a reflection on women's maternal abilities, for example, is an emphasis not simply on the production of children but the giving birth to all manner of things, 'love, desire, language, art, social things, political things, religious things' (Irigaray 1985: 18). Women's maternal nature—which under patriarchy has been reduced to one function alone, a function which both serves and perpetuates patriarchy—becomes symbolic of a multinatured identity which patriarchy cannot contain. Similarly while the Pope partially grounds his maternal understanding of women in their physiology, Irigaray points out that woman's embodiment actually teaches her that she is not reducible to a physical mother alone—for she has a clitoris, an organ whose only purpose is the production of pleasure. The clitoris symbolizes women's *jouissance*, women's joy, delight and difference that leads to a form of knowledge unafraid of difference and diversity (Irigaray 1985). Beattie points out that the clitoris actually disrupts John Paul's theology of the body for it severs the 'natural' connection between sex and reproduction and places pleasure centrally: 'if the phallus can symbolise a culture of domination, aggression and power, the clitoris might even symbolise a culture that celebrates playfulness and nurtures small delights in the loving and patient encounters of daily life' (Beattie 1997: 180).

Ironically, the male body has also been problematized in the Christian tradition. With bodiliness being associated with femininity and destabilization, the male body becomes an object to be controlled by the rational will, just as female bodies must be controlled by the male will. And so it is the perfectly controlled, hard ('softness' being associated with femininity) male body which has been idealized in Christian theology (Nelson 1992b: 93-104).

The body then must be regarded as something to be redeemed, as the Christian tradition has always maintained, though from our vantage point we might say that what it needs to be redeemed from is not so much the concupiscence feared by Augustine, Aquinas and Pope John Paul II as a patriarchal construction and interpretation of embodiment. But the body must also be reclaimed as a site of resistance and epistemology. Such an epistemology and the theology it produces will be radically different from anything we have encountered in this survey of the Christian tradition because a true consciousness of embodiment involves a recognition of one's situatedness in history, culture and therefore of the particularity of one's vision. However, the issues that theologians of the body face today—issues of gender, desire, change and decay, issues of difference and meaning—are all ones familiar to our ancestors in faith. We may tackle these issues with different tools and different horizons but we are involved in the same project to make sense of a difficult, slippery and ambiguous reality in the light of faith.

Chapter Four

The Sacred Body?
Women, Spirituality and Embodiment

In Chapter 2 it was argued that, while Christian theology may have managed to avoid a terminal collapse into body/soul dualism, the persistent ambiguity towards the body that has haunted the Christian tradition is grounded (at the very least) in an ambiguity towards the female body. Foucault's description of the body as a site upon which institutions exercise power and as a site of resistance to that power both reflected and proudly influenced the understanding of the histories and possible futures of the female body in all types of feminism (Foucault 1978).[1] But it is perhaps in thealogy that the most sustained and creative analysis of

---

1. Rosemarie Tong isolates seven types of feminism currently extant in the western world: liberal feminism which is grounded in the Enlightenment project and concerned with the attainment of equal rights for women; Marxist feminism which locates the oppression of women in the economic structures of capitalism and their liberation in a socialist order; radical feminism which is concerned with the wholesale subversion and destruction of patriarchy through a reclaiming and resacralizing of women's bodies; psychological feminism which locates women's oppression in the Oedipus complex; existential feminism which characterizes woman under patriarchy as the Other whose meaning is determined for her by man. Liberation lies in becoming a self through the rejection of male determination. Socialist feminism has endeavoured to synthesize all the previously mentioned theories because it recognizes the complexities of women's oppression—women are alienated in many different ways. Postmodern feminism draws attention to differences among and between women. It accuses the other types of feminism of failing to pay sufficient attention to differences of race, class, sexuality, and economic status among women. Too often feminism has simply reflected the world of the white, heterosexual, middle-class, western woman. Feminism must not fall into the universalizing tendencies of patriarchal thought: there is no one true reality but many, not one feminism but many feminisms. Feminist theologians can be found in each of these types of feminism (Tong 1989).

women's bodies has taken place.[2] Thealogy differs from Christian feminism in that it endeavours to begin its reflection in a space beyond patriarchal religion. This branch of feminism can be difficult to get a handle on because it is so diverse.[3] Basically, thealogy maintains that patriarchy has de-sacralized and demonized women's bodies, and it seeks to resacralize women's bodies: 'in thealogy a woman's embodied finitude is holy in that it belongs to the intramundane processes of divine creativity' (Raphael 1996: 23). The divine is often named in thealogy as 'the Goddess'. This term is deliberately slippery (which reflects thealogy's aversion to dogma) and can refer to a whole number of things: the Great Mother (a biological fertility symbol) or the Great Goddess (a metaphysical symbol of cosmic oneness); the ontological priority of a divine female cosmogonic principle; a private sense of the divinity of the female self; a purely psychotherapeutic symbol of self-affirmation; a conflation of the qualities of numerous ancient goddesses; or some degree of all these... (Raphael 1996: 246).

Some spiritual feminists are Goddess 'realists', some are not and some are some of the time, but all agree that the power of the divine is radically immanent and that there is no radical dualism (or even a 'soft', ambivalent dualism) between body and spirit, public and private, or between divine and human. The central claim of thealogy is that women image the divine in the embodied reality of their daily lives including the bodily changes and processes that patriarchal religion has found so difficult to deal with—menstruation, birth, sexual activity, menopause, ageing and death. The Goddess is often represented as the three phases of womanhood—virgin, mother and crone. Many women have found this identification between their own embodied reality and the divine extremely empowering and healing against a cultural background which still finds women's embodiment problematic in many respects (Christ 1979; Harvey 1997: 69-86; Long 1994).

A key claim of thealogy is that one of the fundamental mechanisms used by patriarchy to profane women's bodies is reversal, the most obvious example being the myth of a woman being born from the body of a man in Genesis 2, but it is also evident in the Church's confining of the tasks of birthing (through baptism) and feeding (through the eucharist)

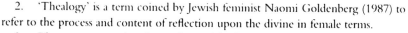

2. 'Thealogy' is a term coined by Jewish feminist Naomi Goldenberg (1987) to refer to the process and content of reflection upon the divine in female terms.

3. The most comprehensive analysis of thealogy is Raphael 1996. In this chapter we rely heavily on Raphael's study.

to male 'fathers'. And so 'reversing the reversals' is at the heart of the thealogical method. It is evident in the way that thealogists read ancient patriarchal texts. Along with most feminist theologians they adopt a hermeneutic of suspicion, exposing the power relations reflected in and established by the texts. In patriarchal texts women have usually been silenced: they do not speak to us as subjects of their own discourse but it is often possible through the silences or fissures in a text to pick up dim echoes of their voices. What is read is not what the text says but what it does not say. Imagination is therefore a key tool in the development of thealogy and is also evident in the creation of the grand narrative of the origins of patriarchy. This metanarrative is a fiction (it cannot be verified and has often been questioned) but it nevertheless functions as truth in that it generates future biophilic possibilities.

One of the dualisms perpetuated by patriarchy is the dualism of sacred/profane. Women's bodies have been placed on the profane side of the equation, with no escape possible:

> women are excluded from the powerful male cults and so whatever they use or issue from their bodies is more or less profane [because the profane is that which is for non-cultic, everyday use]. And the profane is defined as that which is beneath divine notice and so cannot be consecrated to the cult—the very cult women have been excluded from. And so it goes on (Raphael 1996: 38-39).

Mary Daly has noted that the word 'profane' is derived from two Latin words meaning 'before the temple'. She therefore invites women to embrace the profanity.

> Feminist profanity is the wild realm of the sacred as it was/is before being caged into the temple of Father Time. It is free time/space ... Since it is not confined within the walls of any spatial or temporal temple, it transcends the 'accepted' dichotomies between the sacred and the profane (Daly 1978: 48).

Thealogy reverses this sacred/profane construction. So whereas patriarchy profanes menstrual and post-partum blood, associating it with death and disorder whilst sacralizing the shedding of (particularly male) blood through torture, martyrdom and war, thealogy lays hold of the obvious but feared power associated with the bleeding woman in patriarchal discourse but reverses its meaning. It becomes a life-affirming power. A clear example of this reversal in action is the way that menstrual blood was used by the women living in the peace camp at Greenham Common. Drawing power from the patriarchal suspicion that contact with menstrual blood makes men impotent sexually and in the practice of war, women soaked clothes in their menstrual blood and tied them to the gates and fences of the nuclear airforce base. Here the deadly power of menstrual blood was reversed to become destructive of the ultimate lethal powers of patriarchy and therefore life-giving and sustaining (Amberston 1991: 60-61). Menstrual blood is also sometimes saved and used to fertilize gardens by thealogists. Whereas modern patriarchy profanes menstrual blood by denying its existence and providing an array of products and images designed to keep women in the workplace and sexually accessible to men, thealogists often use their menstrual period as a 'sabbath' time in which they recharge their energies with what they believe to be creative power unleashed by and in the bleeding (Raphael 1996: 196-203). At the same time, thealogists name as profane the shedding of blood through violence or war, for it is an affront to the biophilic, erotic power of the sacred.

In Chapter 2 it was noted that what has disturbed theologians and philosophers most about women's bodies is their state of constant flux and change, and which was taken to symbolize disorder and chaos that constantly threatens to engulf and destroy patriarchal, sacred order. Women shared this flaw with all matter. This belief was dynamically interrelated with a construction of the divine as a static, unchangeable god of law and order who is ultimately pure spirit. Yet, post-modern science and philosophy has blown apart this cosmology. Science has demonstrated that there is no dualism between spirit or energy and matter and that matter itself is neither fixed nor predictable. The whole of the universe is in fact a complex web of interrelationality in a constant state of flux. The universe and the organisms which make it up are chaotic, in a process of deforming and reforming (Raphael 1996: 245-56). Process theology and thealogy relocate the divine at the core of this universe. The power of the sacred is not a static power of law and order but a dynamic, energy that disturbs and disrupts the necrophilic patterns of human ordering and prevents the sterility of idolatry by keeping everything in a creative flux (Whitehead 1929 and 1938). This paradigm shift allows for a revaluing of female bodies as embodiments of the sacred power of the universe, in their very being disturbing and distorting the deadly powers of patriarchy. The chaos theory also allows for a new spiritual understanding of activism and ritual. The famous 'butterfly effect' (whereby a butterfly flapping its wings can set off a chain of effects that alters the weather on the other side of the globe) can help us

to understand how ritual, prayer and prophetic protest such as was practised at Greenham Common and at other peace camps can have world-
changing effects, although those effects may not be obviously or even
logically traceable to the ritual or action. The individual and group body
therefore becomes a vitally important and effective mediatrix of sacred
power.

From Silence to Speech

Thealogy seeks to rescue the female body from the desacralizing which
took place in the Judaeo-Christian context of the sacralizing of male
bodiliness and from the modern desacralizing of the female body
through its construction as a body of flesh available for the enjoyment of
men. The Jewish and Christian traditions, by playing their part in
defining female embodiment in terms of the absence of reason, thereby
removing it from public space, and in constructing a cosmology and
theology which reflects and legitimates this fabrication of the female
body, have 'rendered female flesh dumb' (Raphael 1996: 81). Thealogy
seeks to hear female flesh into speech by both exposing the myriad ways
in which it is silenced and subverting them. In the modern western
world the most obvious and universal means by which female flesh is
'disciplined' is through the culture of dieting. Raphael points out that it
is no coincidence that the growth in weight-watching classes took place
at exactly the same time as the growth of feminist consciousness-raising
groups. In the latter, 'women gathered to support one another and
develop their public presence and power'; in the former 'women gathered to support one another and *reduce* their presence and restrain their
power' (Raphael 1996: 86). And, indeed, several feminist theorists have
argued that the diet culture has been a particularly effective part of the
backlash against feminism that we have witnessed in the past two
decades, a backlash which has been precipitated by the arrival of some
women in previously male-only zones of employment (Faludi 1992 and
Wolf 1991). It is the women who are most likely to enter into male
space—white, middle-class women—who are most affected by the
pressure to diet (though all women are put under some pressure). The
marketing of special foods, classes, gyms etc are all aimed at this socio-
economic group, although no women remain unaffected. Women are
pressurized to achieve a weight which is usually at least one stone
beneath their natural weight (Wolf 1991). The ideal woman's body
therefore conveys physical weakness, whereas men exercise to increase

their strength. Female body building may have become more popular in recent years but all that is produced by it, according to these feminist theorists, is an imitation of the male body. It does nothing to challenge male power or aggression. Women who are literally starving to death— Raphael draws attention to the shocking fact that many women on weight-loss programmes consume less calories than the Jews in the Nazi extermination camps (Raphael 1996: 88)—simply do not have the energy to become involved in feminism. They are taught to judge themselves and other women in terms of shape. A constant regime of self-surveillance and discipline alienates a woman from her bodiliness and from other women. Dieting is perhaps the most obvious and usual necrophilic practice women perform. Burning off weight or flesh is a way of sacrificing one's own person as burnt offering: literally, a holo-caust. And when, as in spiritual feminism, that weight/flesh also gener-ates sacral energy, its burning becomes redolent of the witchburnings where female flesh was burnt off to liberate and redeem the soul (Raphael 1996: 90).

The women who are locked into a never-ending spiral of dieting are not in the same position as those mediaeval women whose fasting was motivated by the desire and need to subvert male power in the Church. Yet both sets of women, according to the thealogists, are ultimately vic-tims of the patriarchal tendency to drain women of their bodiliness and therefore their sacred energy.

The patriarchal system uses 'perfectly' shaped women to peddle a deadly parade of reversals: women are advised to eat 'good for you' foods which have been produced in ways that poison the earth, while being warned against eating (among other things) biophilicly grown foods because they cause bloating (Raphael 1996: 94). Both earth and female flesh are reduced to the status of dead matter to be formed and consumed by male will.

The language of the diet culture is a curious quasi-religious language. Food is presented as sinful. Public confession and surveillance, as well as private discipline and ritual, are used to build up will power and those who succeed in suppressing desire are transported into the sacred sphere of the elect. Indeed, some feminists have argued that the diet culture has taken over from religion the role of disciplining the female body (Wolf 1991: 88). Raphael explores the way in which the ideal of the perfect female body is rooted deep within the Christian tradition. In the letter to the Ephesians the Church is presented as a female body, the perfect female body, completely obedient to her Lord, Christ, and 'without spot or wrinkle or any such thing' (Eph. 5.27). The ramification of this theology would seem to be that the 'non-perfect' female body, individual or corporate, could never be sacramental, it could never bear the sacred presence of Christ. It is profane. This is further reinforced by the construction of Mary as uniquely physically and morally perfect (Raphael 1996: 97-98).

Although the author of the letter to the Ephesians does not mention body size when painting a picture of the perfect female form, the references to spot and wrinkle convey images of ageing and therefore of a natural change and perhaps a natural 'filling out'. The Church as the bride of Christ must not be susceptible to change, to flux, there must be no spare flesh on her. The aged, wrinkled and large body is profaned. The large woman in contemporary culture is portrayed as a woman out of control, on the brink of death, grossly self-indulgent. So the large woman is portrayed as weak, the weak as strong, the starving are portrayed as healthy, the well-fed as diseased. Thealogy seeks to examine and reverse this reversal. The large woman is indeed, out of control, out of patriarchal control. In her resistance to the various forms of patriarchal forms of self-surveillance she comes to symbolize the 'formlessness', the chaos that patriarchy so fears. And so it punishes her by representing her in terms that mean that, like all profane objects, she is only for 'common use', often confined to lowly menial jobs. She is ejected from public space, 'like old women whose bodies are also marked by organic change…those women who will not render themselves invisible (slimmed down or shrunk) are simply removed from sight. Their naturalness is too fearful to look upon' (Raphael 1996: 99). The media does not represent them except in the most negative terms, nor do they tend to end up in positions of responsibility and prestige. Thealogy celebrates the sacred flux and change of the universe, it will not endorse the freezing of the female form in a state of adolescent immaturity and powerlessness. The power of the Goddess is a biophilic power which is expressed in food, hospitable, enveloping flesh, sexual expression which does not mirror and enact the patriarchal order and the power and energy of matter.

Different Bodies

For thealogians, then, the body is a site of resistance to and transformation of patriarchal reality. This site is a sacred site because it mediates the biophilic power of the divine, thwarting all attempts to control and subdue it. But not all feminists find this approach to the body helpful or convincing. Both secular feminists and feminist theologians have exposed the ideas it espouses to critical analysis.

Alison Jagger, commenting on secular radical feminism, makes some points which can also be applied to thealogy. She has noted that, while radical feminists have done more than any other group of feminists to ground feminist analysis in a thorough-going materialism and thereby taken the female body, its sexuality, its childbearing and reproductive powers and its representation, into the political domain, they seem ultimately to take an essentialist and deterministic attitude to human biology. Jagger points out that human biology is not a static given, it is in flux and changes as it interacts with other forces. In some cultures women are as tall, narrow-hipped and broad as men. We can explain the fact that in the West women tend to be smaller than men by the social forces of patriarchy. We have already examined the effects of the modern diet culture but long before that women were expected to yield the best food to their menfolk. In other words we have to recognize that there is a complex relationship between biology and environment that produces different bodies in different contexts (Jagger 1983: 249-302). Women's bodies are different. One of the most persistent criticisms of thealogy is that it is blind to class and racial differences between women and reflects white, western, middle-class experience of the female body.

Thealogy is not the only branch of feminism to be vulnerable to such a charge. Feminist theology and indeed body theology in general have often proved all too willing to use the writings of black women to advance their arguments without paying sufficient attention to the context out of which the women write and the differences between the experiences of black and white women. Thus white writers engage in the same kind of exploitation and colonization of black people as the religio-socio-political systems they claim to want to subvert. The writings of Alice Walker and Toni Morrison have been particularly vulnerable to appropriation and exploitation. Baby Suggs, a character in Morrison's *Beloved*, is oft quoted for her words on flesh:

> 'Here', she said, 'in this place, we flesh; flesh that weeps, laughs; flesh that dances on bare feet in the grass. Love it. Love it hard. Yonder they do not love your flesh. They despise it... You got to love it. You... This is flesh I'm talking about here. Flesh that needs to be loved' (Morrison 1987: 88-98).

Walker's character Shug in *The Colour Purple* is also cited for her theological reflections which seem to express the radical immanence that characterizes radical feminism's view of the divine:

> You come into the world with God. But only them that search for it inside find it. And sometimes it just manifests itself even if you not looking, or don't know what you are looking for... It ain't a picture show. It ain't something you can look at apart from anything else, including yourself. I believe God is everything, say Shug. Everything that is or ever was or ever will be. And when you can feel that, and be happy to feel that, you've found it (Walker 1982: 167).

Yet, as Susan Thistlethwaite has noted, a superficial and exploitative use of selective passages from womanists[4] simply does violence to black women's experience which often grates against the construction of the sacred female body in radical feminism (Thistlethwaite 1989). Womanist attitudes to embodiment are in fact deeply ambiguous. This is because, at least in the history of the USA, it is not true that all women have always stood for nature and been treated like the earth, exploited and raped. In the USA it is black women who have been identified with nature and white women with culture. This both explains white women's desire to reclaim their embodiedness and relationship to nature and black women's deep ambiguity towards nature. Black women writers do share with thealogians an awareness of the independence of and interdependence with nature, but 'the powerful spiritual forces...are deranged in complex patterns by race, sex and class; and these derangements and displacements cannot be overcome by sheer mental process' (Thistlethwaite 1989: 71). For many womanists nature is fallen, evil is a reality, as is sin, which cannot be simply wished away and indeed both evil and sin are often at the root of resistance and creativity in black communities. Black women relate to nature and embodiment in a complex way because they are by and large excluded from the post-patriarchal harmonious world that spiritual feminists create for themselves.

The Asian feminist theologian Kwok Pui-Lan has drawn attention to the fact that the language of the erotic, which is found in both feminist theology and thealogy and was first formulated by a black woman (Lorde) is virtually absent from the theologizing of non-white women beyond the shores of Europe and the USA. This is because in places like

4. 'Womanist' is a term chosen by black women to emphasize the differences between them and white feminists.

Thailand and the Philippines the female body is still constructed primarily in terms of a body to be sold. In these cultures 'flesh' constitutes the 'flesh trade' and the 'erotic' the power of men over women's bodies (Kwok Pui-Lan 1994: 63-76). Female embodiment is experienced as tragic by non-white, non-western feminists in a manner that white feminists cannot even begin to imagine.

Korean theologian Chung Hyun Kyung points out that pain and suffering must be the epistemological starting points for Asian women's theological reflection because this is their reality: 'Asian women's epistemology is an *epistemology from the broken body*, a broken body longing for healing and wholeness' (Chung Hyun Kyung 1990: 39). Certainly there is plenty of material in Asian women's theology that would resonate with thealogians: an understanding of God as radically immanent, whose creativity is experienced by women in their own creativity, a God in process, a maternal God. The power of this God excites in women a biophilic power which will enable women 'to be the sun again'. Chung Hyun Kyung takes that phrase from a poem by a Japanese woman, Hiratsuka Raicho, who claims that 'originally woman was the sun. She was an authentic person. But now woman is the moon' (Chung Hyun Kyung 1990: 51-52). This association of authentic womanhood with the sun rather than with the shifting cycle of the moon demonstrates how differently eastern women view the world. The struggle to be sun again certainly involves renegotiating traditional images and doctrines from the perspective of being Asian women, but speaking out of the broken body again produces a complex theology of multiple images because these women are acutely aware of the need for redemption of the body, of nature, of male/female relations. Thealogy regards the figure of the Virgin Mary as the creation of patriarchal desire, a plastic, 'made up' ideal woman used to further alienate women from their desires and bodies (though some believe it is possible to redeem the original goddess figure from the doll into which she has been moulded). Asian women's theology, while recognizing that this is the way that Mary has been 'read', reads her in a different way. For Indonesian theologian Marianne Katoppo Mary's perpetual virginity can be read as referring to her perpetual resistance to patriarchy. She is a virgin in the sense that she defines herself and refuses to allow herself to be defined by men. The virgin birth then becomes for Korean theologian Han Kuk Yum the beginning of the end of the patriarchal order. Mary also co-operates with God in the redemption of humanity, the very act of co-operation being redemptive, 'In order to achieve salvation, we, like Mary, have to accept our own redemption freely. Mary shows us that without our co-operation, redemption of humanity is impossible' (Chung Hyung Kyung 1990: 83).

Asian women's bodies are broken bodies, they cannot simply get up and walk out of that pain and so they redeem it using the language, images and resources around them. This is a characteristic also found in black women's theology, according to Thistlethwaite, which resists white theology/thealogy's tendency to push towards one understanding and naming of the divine. Black theology has a long history of using gender-inclusive imagery for God and it has an equally long history of imaging Jesus in ways that have been sustaining and liberating for black women. The tendency of *some* theologians and thealogians simply to dismiss such beliefs as necrophilic for women demonstrates an astonishing arrogance which associates (some) white women's experience with 'truth'. Beverly Wildung Harrison finds Mary Daly's call for women to journey into the 'Otherworld' of 'Womenspace' deeply disturbing, not only because many women because of their economic, racial and social situation are simply unable to step outside (even for a few moments a day) this world of patriarchy, but because 'for the feminist… *life itself, and the embodied world of flesh and blood*, are the true gifts of God' (Harrison 1990: 197). It is those who are oppressed and marginalized who are closer to 'the real, material conditions of life' than those who benefit from the structures of patriarchy. A moral feminist ethic must be based in the everyday life of the most marginalized women according to Harrison, in the (broken) flesh and blood of those to whom Daly's spiral galaxies are completely beyond view.

Thistlethwaite also encourages white feminist theologians and thealogians to examine their use of process theology. She points out that process theology and philosophy were not invented by feminist women but by liberal Protestant men and that fact alone should caution us against an uncritical acceptance. Indeed, she believes that 'process theology imports into theological discourse a dualistic world view under the guise of relationality' (Thistlethwaite 1989: 87). This dualistic world view manifests itself in the way in which process theologians appear to identify human mental processes with the image of God. Its vision for an ever more progressive future is the gradual resolving of differences into a harmonious system. This higher mental synthesis enables us to transcend the world and reconstitute ourselves. Thistlethwaite points out that this drives a wedge between the mental process and the material world and it also presupposes a white liberal world of freedom of choice. What does it mean to a poor woman or a battered woman to transcend the world and reconstitute herself?

> This is as inadequate in developing a trenchant critique of the social origins of sin, and the social sources of salvation, as is the theological perspective that places God outside the world and reduces God's capacity for self-revelation to dropping stones on us. Perhaps the former is even more inadequate because it succeeds in homogenizing judgment and reducing sin to maladjustment, eviscerating the capacity for a trenchant social criticism (Thistlethwaite 1989: 88-90).

Thistlethwaite believes that white women have been socialized by American culture to provide the cohesive glue holding society together, they therefore have been socialized into connectivity. However, the purpose of this connectivity was to keep the dominant white culture dominant and Thistlethwaite firmly believes that an uncritical dive by white feminists into images of webs, matrix and connections is in danger of simply perpetuating 'the white-assumed privilege of owning the world' (Thistlethwaite 1989: 91). Thistlethwaite does not want to deny that there are connections between women and that it is possible to reflect upon them, but these real connections will only emerge through a direct confrontation with 'the terror of difference', a willingness to meet the embodied Other. The implications for feminist theology and theaology are important—theo/alogical reflection must be grounded in the real, material embodied experience of different women, this in turn will require a centring of theologies of sin and redemption as we confront both our pasts and our involvement in its colonial legacies. The construction of the divine must contain a sufficient Otherness constantly to call us away from an easy language of relationality. Yet much theaology and feminist theology seems to deny the otherness of the divine, totally collapsing her into human experience.

Pam Lunn also raises questions about the ultimate liberatory value of theaology and its attitude to the body. She doubts the effectiveness of a simple reversal of the patriarchal evaluation of the connection between women, embodiment and the earth:

> The assertion of their own worth by members of an oppressed group within a society will not inevitably lead the dominant group(s) to change their value hierarchies, their behaviour or their symbol systems, whether the assertion be 'Black is beautiful', 'female is powerful' or 'women's

bodies are sacred'. The danger for any subordinate group which seeks to re-assign the value labels *within* the dominant symbolic structure is that attempts to effect change may be merely ignored, neutralised or co-opted. A much harder task is the struggle to create new symbol systems which genuinely give voice or vision to emerging perceptions in the culture (Lunn 1993: 28).

Lunn has also questioned the concept of female sacral power mediated through the bodies of women. She notes that the impression can sometimes be given that this power is pure/innocent power, untainted by patriarchy, but the exercise of power by women even within the 'Otherworldly' space of Womenspace has proved problematic and women have been shown to be not immune from the abusive use of power.[5] It may well be that women have not yet learnt how to exercise power but if that is the case we need to learn that power is always mediated through our histories and cultural and social contexts—the webs of patriarchy. Women may site their bodies in places on the boundaries of patriarchy, as the women of the peace camps have done, and there their bodies become symbols and sites of resistance to patriarchy. In this space power moves differently, it may move in ways that are liberating and empowering for the women involved but it is never innocent, it is never purified of patriarchy.

Critics of thealogy accuse it of failing to take sufficient account of embodied differences between women. The need for white women in particular to take account of the embodied experiences of black and Asian women is particularly urgent, for what their experience teaches us is the need to hold on to a transcendent as well as an immanent aspect of the divine, a sacred power which is both with us but also 'other' to us and 'beyond' us which can summon us to a wider perspective than our own experience of embodiment and which can (with our co-operation) redeem us from our broken, embodied world.

The Disabled God

One group of people who force us to confront issues of difference in embodiment and warn us against an easy romanticizing of 'the body' are persons with disabilities.[6] They also have much to teach those of us yet without physical disabilities about body knowledge:

5.   This point has also been made by Angela West (1995), reflecting on her time at Greenham Common.
6.   A whole variety of terms have been invented by people with disabilities to

The corporeal is for people with disabilities the most real. Unwilling and unable to take our bodies for granted, we attend to the kinesis of knowledge. That is, we become keenly aware that our physical selves determine our perceptions of the social and physical world. These perceptions, like our bodies, are often nonconforming and disclose new categories and models of thinking and being (Eiesland 1994: 31).

One of the most obvious lessons that the disabled body teaches us, if we allow ourselves to learn from it, is the social construction of disability and therefore the body. The disabled body is defined as such against a cultural concept of the abled body which varies from culture to culture. Just as the sexually different have often been accredited with sacred powers outside of western societies so the physically different have often been accorded special status as mediators of the holy. The body is never a stable concept. There are some interesting parallels that can be drawn between the constructions of the disabled body and homosexual body: the association of the unusual with the unnatural and the impure, the medicalization of both conditions which removes them from a social context, the use of this process by people constructed in this way (at least in the West) to produce a reverse discourse in which they make themselves the subject and an increasing interest in the possibilities of gene therapy to do away with these 'abnormalities'. People with disabilities, along with lesbian and gay people and others, have been made into the 'other', the less than fully human, the 'wicked', because their bodies symbolize the disorder which confronts the patriarchal order.

Nancy Eiesland is one of the first theologians to attempt to develop a liberatory theology of disability through an analysis of the lived experience of people with disabilities. She notes that their stories defy both the common perspectives that disability is tragic or only a problem because of other people's misunderstandings or lack of facilities. People with disabilities bespeak the essential contingency of embodiment which can be both a source of grief and a source of creativity. They also understand embodiment in terms very different to that of thealogy (which has tended to take a very 'pure' understanding of embodiment and harbour a distrust of technology). For some, wheelchairs, braces and other appli-

describe themselves in ways that do not conform to their social stereotyping as people less capable than other persons, these include 'persons with disabilities', 'differently abled' and 'physically challenged'. We use the term 'persons with disabilities' because this is the term used by Nancy Eiesland in her ground breaking book (Eiesland 1994).

ances become part of their experience of embodiment. People with disabilities seem to have long grasped what the feminist philosopher Donna Haraway has said to be true of all of us living in the post-modern age—we are cyborgs, 'creatures simultaneously animal and machine, who populate worlds ambiguously natural and crafted' (Haraway 1990. 191). The boundaries between the human body and technology have been blurred, there is no escape back to some kind of 'natural' human body, we have to acknowledge our cyborg nature and renegotiate it. It is perhaps human reluctance to accept its nature as cyborg and the contingency of embodiment that leads to the 'punishment' of the disabled body by the constructing of real and metaphorical barriers to keep it out of public space.

The Church has yet to begin to wrestle with the 'body politics' of the disabled civil rights movement. Eiesland has examined the way in which the Christian tradition has always theologized disability in such a way as to deny disabled people proper access to the social and symbolic life of the Church. Disability has been 'read' to represent an extraordinary relationship with the divine—disability has been linked either with sin or with special righteousness which is tested through an embodied trial. In general a theology of 'virtuous suffering' has predominated in the modern period, linked into a theo-system of charity which has still served to dehumanize people with disability and keep them out of the public domain. The reluctance of some denominations to ordain people with disabilities, while at the same time pledging themselves to make ecclesiastical space more accessible for people with disabilities, demonstrates a failure on the part of the Church to examine its own able-bodiedism fuelled by a tradition which has not constituted the disabled person as a historical moral agent and which therefore always locates the able-bodied at the 'speaking centre'.

Again, there are parallels (though not exact) with the Church's reluctance to ordain openly gay and lesbian people. It is easy to rationalize such decisions because the categories upon which the rationality is built are not open to scrutiny. So the Church makes statements like 'all Christians are disabled in some way' and 'all Christians are sinful', while at the same time denying access to specific groups of 'disabled' (people with disabilities) and 'sinful' (homosexual) people.

Yet Eiesland notes there is within the heart of the Christian tradition a symbol ripe for subversive reclamation and reworking by people with disabilities—the symbol of Christ. For in his resurrected state Christ reveals and is the disabled God, with 'impaired' hands and feet and a pierced side, 'paradoxically, in the very act commonly understood as the transcendence of physical life, God is revealed as tangible, bearing the representation of the body reshaped by injustice and sin into the fullness of the Godhead' (Eiesland 1994: 99-100). The resurrected Christ fulfils the promise of the incarnation that God is with us, embodying the full contingency of human life. And further the disabled God, in revealing true humanity, demonstrates that 'full personhood is fully compatible with the experience of disability' (Eiesland 1994: 100). Jesus the disabled God is neither Lord nor suffering servant but 'survivor', who embraces the ambiguity of life and embodiment without retreating into despair. As survivor the disabled God does not will connectivity and interdependence from a position of privilege but from a position of need.

> This symbol points not to a utopian vision of hope as the erasure of all human contingency, historically or eternally, for that would be to erase our bodies, our lives. Rather it is a liberatory realism that maintains a clear recognition of the limits of our bodies and an acceptance of limits as the truth of being human. This liberatory realism also calls for a realization of the necessity of a social and interpersonal transformation that does not surrender to cynicism and defeatism any more than the limits of our bodies suggest that we should do nothing. It locates our hope in justice as access and mutuality, a justice that removes the barriers which constrain our bodies, keep us excluded, and intend to humiliate us. It also situates our hope in the reality of our existence as ones with dignity and integrity. Hope is the recollection and projection that even our nonconventional bodies, which oftentimes dissatisfy and fail us, are worth the living. It is knowing that the so-called 'curses' sometimes feel like blessings (Eiesland 1994: 103).

Eiesland relates an 'epiphany' in which she saw God 'in a sip-puff wheelchair' mostly used by quadriplegics, a survivor God who is also, to use Haraway's imagery, a cyborg. Perhaps disabled theology has given us both the God and understanding of embodiment that we need at the turning of the centuries, a theology grounded in the profoundly ambiguous and fluid reality of embodiment which subverts attempts to produce a universal theory and demands that we take responsibility for our use of technology rather than simply demonize it. The disabled, cyborg God reveals herself not in reproduction but in the regeneration and reconstitution of the boundaries of this world in which most of us have to live all the time. As Haraway says, 'It means both building and destroying machines, identities, categories, relationships, spaces, stories.

Although both are bound in the spiral dance, I would rather be a cyborg than a goddess' (Haraway 1990: 223). In truth, few of us have any choice. And perhaps the image of the disabled God will help us deal with the hard questions to which Jackie Leach Scully, another disabled theologian, draws our attention:

> Our practical task in theological terms is to do whatever we can to bring about the justice of the kingdom of heaven. It is in accordance with that imperative to affirm the normality of variation and to challenge institutional and individual attitudes that dis-able the different. But we are now able to screen prenatally for certain genetic variations and offer terminations or, in the future, gene therapy to replace some forms of genes with others, and making decisions like these—or deciding not to make them—demands the greatest possible clarity about the point at which we as individuals and societies say: *this* form of embodiment is liveable and should come into being; but *this* form entails so much suffering, that we choose to acknowledge the value of life by preventing that happening (Scully 1998:)

Only a resolutely unromantic attitude to embodiment and a willingness to face up to the terror of otherness will enable us to be equal to that task. It is questionable whether any branch of thealogy or Christian theology has yet provided us with adequate theological tools to attempt it.

Chapter Five

Queering the Body:
The Body in Lesbian and Gay Theology

Thanks largely to the work of Michel Foucault and Mary Douglas, lesbian and gay people have become aware of the way in which their bodies and desires have been constructed in different times and in different cultures. Same-sex desire may have always existed but its interpretation depends upon socio-religio-political understandings of sexual acts and gender relations. Such analysis has enabled lesbian and gay theologians to step into the ongoing and ever circling debate about 'Christianity and homosexuality' and both inform and divert it from the scrap over Scripture into which it has largely plunged, by insisting that issues arising from lesbian and gay experience are examined in the wider context of issues of power, and the ordering of society and gender relations. Why is it that same-sex love is labelled sinful, unlike the social and political forces of capitalism which created and locked men into a form of masculinity based upon competition and drove women into the domestic sphere, preventing them from being active, independent agents in society? Since these forces undoubtedly played their part in the formation of the modern gay and lesbian 'script' (i.e. these sexual identities were constructed to 'take care' of those who resisted such gender constructions) and since they obviously sit uncomfortably with the Christian vision of the reign of God which is based upon friendship, mutual service, radical equality and hospitality, they should surely be subject to theological critique and analysis. Similarly, an awareness of the way that sexuality and gender are constructed and ordered must also oblige Christians to examine the modern structures of heterosexual relations and family life in order to assess their ability to embody the Christian vision of society and relationships (for a full exploration of these issues as they relate to gay male sexuality see Vasey 1995). Lesbian and gay people are only just beginning to find a voice in western society as a whole and in the Church in particular. They have been defined (and rejected) for their desires and for what they do with their bodies to express their desire, so it is little wonder that embodiment has been one of the central themes of the theology emerging from this section of the community.

The Epistemological Flesh

One of the themes that runs throughout both lesbian and gay theology is body knowledge. The body is experienced as a source and site of knowledge whose 'voice' can break through the epistemology of oppression, or as Eve Kosofsky Sedgwick has put it, the epistemology of the closet (Sedgwick 1990). Many writers describe this in deeply personal terms. Gary David Comstock describes the way in which as a teenager his body confirmed and taught him about his 'difference', his persistent resistance to the life of heterosexuality that was mapped out for him. Despite having been told by his family through his brother that masturbation was perfectly acceptable and that he would be fantasizing about women when he did it, he found himself fantasizing about male bodies. He knew nothing about 'homosexuality' as such, his only guide for even being able to imagine a male body against his was his body's 'ache'.

> My body gave evidence, substantiated, formalized, gave expression to that earlier uncertainty—that I wanted/needed to do something that was unexpected and not taught. In spite of social expectations, gender-role socialization, and sex education, my body was determined to have its way; and my decision was, in my fantasies at least, to go with it, to imagine what was not permitted or even available as a model, while living out my daily life as a normal, happy heterosexual adolescent (Comstock 1993: 119).

Melanie May charts her own journey towards acceptance of her grandmother's dictum 'a body knows', in a great deal more detail. Illness as much as desire played a part in awakening her to that knowledge. Problems with her back taught her that 'embodied life is limited life' and that 'to live without an awareness of my limits I would languish, a prisoner to my preoccupation with being perfect, being without failure or flaw' (May 1995: 18). Lying in bed almost dying of complications that followed surgery on her back, May found herself reaching for the telephone, 'my body knew to be alive is to be connected'. Surrounded by bodies, upholding her body, she pulled through (May 1995: 18). Reading Foucault during a period of convalescence she began to understand the extent to which her body had been in bondage to the expectations of society and Church and she began to perceive that connectedness at any price was not real connectedness, some things have to be let go of in order that new life can begin. May believes that it is this terror of 'letting go' that prevents mainstream Christian denominations, most of which appear to be dying, from welcoming and learning from the new ecclesial communities rising around the world and among different groups of people. Their 'letting go' of the disconnection between word and flesh, worship and world which tends to characterize most mainstream Christian denominations is 'giving birth to new forms of human connected in an age of alienation' (May 1995: 39). Also, in proclaiming themselves the Church, these groups lay hold of Jesus' instruction in Mt. 18.18 to the whole Christian community to bind and loose, to become agents of God's power. Every Christian is therefore called into the collective, communal process of deciding what is life-giving, what results in right connection, and what is death-dealing and therefore has to be let go of. If it fails to let go, to die in order to rise to new life, a Church can no longer be considered part of Christ's dying and rising body (May 1995: 39-41). The story of Jesus' transfiguration is for May, as for the Orthodox Church, not a story about God appearing to human beings, but a story of the human becoming part of the divine glory. This is what the Church is called to do: to bear witness in its body to the life of God. It does this most clearly and effectively when it participates with God in the process of binding and loosing, connecting and letting go, rising and dying (May 1995: 41). What is to be feared is not death but death in life, the refusal to let go or connect.

Subsequent experience of breast cancer also taught May about body knowledge. She knew in her 'bones' that she had cancer even when she was attempting to deny it to herself. But the knowledge her body conveyed to her through her breast cancer was even more profound. It taught her about the loss of love in her life, loss which was not caused by the absence of love but by her refusal to accept her own loveableness. She gradually realized that unless she learnt to love herself she would not love others. The great waves of love which washed over her during her treatment gradually began to erode her self-hatred. Her body through the breast, symbol of nurturance, drew attention to the crisis of nurture in her life.

Depression had haunted May from her childhood. Depression that she can now see was induced by a failure to fit into society's construct of a woman's body. She blamed herself for not fitting in and for the depression that ensued. It was only when her illness was properly diagnosed that she was able both to discard her sense of guilt for her condition and her concern at how others would react to it. All this has enabled her to come into a state of Real Presence.

> I live, and think, in my body, no longer alienated or abstracted as I have been most of my life. I delight in my body's desires—sensory and sexual. I savour the pleasure of aromas and beauty, of taste and touch. I honour what my body knows. More particularly, I live, and think, in my female body. I have come out as a woman! I come out convinced that what matters, for men as well as women, in the face of society's stultifying code of conformity is for each one to affirm our own uniqueness and our finitude, so we are able to respect and risk being changed by the reality of otherness (May 1995: 68).

This bodily presence she believes is also an experience of divine presence. Divine presence makes others alive, in this sense it is authoritative and such life can only emerge from a body that is self-affirming. A body which is not present to itself, which makes a person absent in their presence, is death-dealing to itself and those around it. It can feel no connection, it is not able to be open to otherness.

An essential part of May's struggle to be present in her body was the decision to come out as a lesbian. The alternative for May, the silence of 'passing' as heterosexual, is a sin of omission, 'I omit myself from being the fullness of the image of God as God created me to be. I thereby put God's glory at risk as well as my own being, for…God's glory is dimmed whenever and wherever women and men created in God's image are diminished or violated' (May 1995: 83). The truth sets a lesbian or gay person free to be fully alive and therefore to incarnate fully God's glory. We need to lay our bodies bare, to risk vulnerability in a world which is so often powered by deception, because only thus can the real presence of the divine be manifest. Truth, as Pilate did not appreciate, is not abstract but always manifest in the bodies in front of you. It demands relationship.

And so May has learnt through her body to practise resurrection. She has come to relate to her body not simply as a symbol or as a mass of matter on which social constructions are written but as an active knower, which is in a constant process of change and which is finite.

She has experienced her body, as many other lesbian and gay people have, as a source and site of resistance against 'terror and tyranny' and a source of what she calls 'trespass', for body knowledge trespasses over all sorts of boundaries including the boundaries established by traditional academic theology. Here she echoes Marcella Althaus Reid who describes feminist theology as the process of 'plotting desires', which is as subversive an activity as it sounds because women's desires have been subject to patriarchal law and order. Plotting and trespassing are part of the same process: plotting female desire leads to a trespassing of the boundaries of hetero-patriarchy (Althaus Reid 1997).

Carter Heyward thinks along very similar lines to May. She believes that part of the resistance to lesbian and gay voices that is manifest in many Christian denominations springs from a fear of 'knowing consciously—intellectually, ethically, and responsibly—what our bodies know already and what our corporate body also knows… We know we want and need and deeply desire connection… In essence, we yearn for genuine *mutual* relation' (Heyward 1995: 115). As we have already observed Heyward follows the black lesbian feminist poet and philosopher, Audre Lorde, in identifying this deep body knowledge with *eros*. For Lorde *eros* is the power of true feeling, 'an internal sense of satisfaction', which once experienced drives us towards its realization in every aspect of our lives.

> The considered phrase, 'It feels right to me', acknowledges the strength of the erotic into a true knowledge, for what that means and feels is the first and most powerful guiding light towards any understanding. And understanding is a handmaiden which can only wait upon, or clarify, that knowledge, deeply born. The erotic is the nurturer or nursemaid of all our deepest knowledge (Lorde 1994: 77).

Erotic power is evident in the sharing of joy with another and in the bodily act of creativity, when released into our lives it prevents us from simply accepting oppression and the numbness that necessarily comes with it. The erotic propels us out of a sense of powerlessness but it also prevents the use and abuse of others. It demands that we feel, that we are (as May would put it) present to ourselves. Heyward identifies the erotic with God, a sacred power moving among us as the power of connection and mutuality in relation (Heyward 1989). When people live out of that sacred power incarnating it in their life and relationships, they may be said to be 'godding'. Heyward does not underestimate the obstacles that prevent us from godding. In a world and Church which constructs power in terms of 'power-over' and associates that power with 'big, hard and up' masculinity that values sensation above feeling, experience of and fear of abuse alienates from erotic power and from the relationships of mutuality and justice which it reproduces. Yet, she maintains, we still yearn for this power in every aspect of our lives, including our sex, work and Church lives.

The danger of this epistemology of the flesh that has emerged from lesbian and gay theology is that it might give the impression of replacing the disembodied, autonomous self with the disembodied, autonomous body which is a reliquary for a pure form of knowledge unsullied by cultural constructions. If the primary lesson of our renewed awareness of our embodiment is the situatedness and particularity of all knowledge then we cannot exclude our body knowledge from that. It cannot be 'pure' knowledge. Perhaps the best way to avoid this trap is to follow the path of Foucault, who vigorously contested the view that power simply operated in a top–down pattern. He argued that in every exercise of power there are 'points of resistance' to be found all over the network of power,

> each of them a special case: resistances that are possible, necessary, improbable; others that are spontaneous, savage, solitary, concerted, rampant, or violent; still others that are quick to compromise, interested, or sacrificial; by definition, they can only exist in the strategic field of power relations. But this does not mean that they are only a reaction or rebound, forming with respect to the basic domination an underside that is in the end always passive, doomed to perpetual defeat (Foucault 1978: 96).

It is therefore inevitable in a society which devalues the body that the body should become a site of resistance and in a society which seeks to impose a system of compulsory heterosexuality that there should be reaction against it and resistance to it. Emily Martin has suggested that the further a group of people are from the centre of dominating power the more possible it is for them to subvert the hegemonic interpretations which are imposed upon our lives in myriad and complex ways (Martin 1989). A *cautious* identification between the power of the sacred and the resurrection of these 'subjugated knowledges' is therefore possible but it must always be cautious and self-consciously partial. Foucault has driven home to us the fluidity and dynamism of power which means that we are always obliged to listen to the voices of resistance in our own practice and theorizing of knowledge.

One group of people who have often been studiously ignored by lesbian and gay people, or even kicked away for politically expedient reasons, are transsexual persons. Yet, perhaps no other group in society represents resistant bodily knowledge as clearly as this one and perhaps no other group warns more against romanticising embodiment. The transsexual experience of embodiment is tragic, it is an experience of gender dysphoria. Lesbian and gay people, along with many feminists, have often found transsexualism difficult to understand and empathize with for a number of reasons. It can often appear that the whole theory of transsexualism is based on a dualism between mind and body: 'a woman's mind trapped in a man's body' or vice versa. Transsexual theory can also appear to encourage the sort of biological essentialism that has made life so difficult for gay people and women. It is often argued by feminists and others that transsexualism is simply the result of a rigid, patriarchal social construction of gender. No doubt there is truth in this—although there may be plenty of other contributing factors—but the simple recognition of this will not magically spirit away the phenomenon of gender dysphoria. We have already noted that feminist theology has begun to move away from a disembodied social constructionism to a more nuanced, embodied approach to gender which recognizes the part that the body plays in its construction. Moira Gatens employs the concept of the 'imaginary body' to illustrate this point. We all inherit from our immediate social and cultural environments an understanding of the meaning of our bodies and the bodies of others, we learn this through the way that the body is talked about and through various social and institutional practices. We acquire a gender identity in response to this 'imaginary body' (Gatens 1991: 139-57). Yet, transsexuals, somehow and for whatever reasons, resist this imaginary body, their whole embodied selves resist the classifications that the imaginary body seeks to impose. For this they are punished by society in all manner of means. It is far too simplistic to characterize transgendered persons as people who want to change sex, as Leslie Feinberg attempted to explain to a reporter. In response to a question about current identity Feinberg replied,

> I am transgendered. I was born female, but my masculine gender expression is seen as male. It is not my sex that defines me, and it's not my gender expression. It's the fact that my gender expression appears to be at odds with my sex... It's the social contradiction between the two that defines me (Feinberg 1996: 101).

The reporter's response 'So you're a *third* sex?' is a typical response, deflecting attention away from the fact that transsexuality actually serves to undermine the whole notion of both sex and gender as they are currently constructed. Transgendered persons should not be punished by feminists or by lesbian and gay people for choosing a sexual and gender identity in a context which will actually not allow you to do anything else. Beyond the frontiers of the western world, transgendered persons have been found occupying highly honoured spiritual positions as mediators of the divine, their transcendence of gender being related to their ability to transcend the divide between the spiritual and earthly (Williams 1992).

Victoria Kolakowski is one of the first to reflect theologically on the basis of her experience of being a transgendered person. She finds in the Hebrew and Christian Scriptures a class of persons who bear a 'family resemblance' not only to transgendered persons but also to lesbian and gay people, because they were a class created and then marginalized by the structuring of gender and society in terms of reproduction. This class consists of eunuchs (Kolakowski 1997: 10-31).[1] Kolakowski shares this approach with lesbian theologian Nancy Wilson, who notes that eunuchs in the Hebrew Scriptures often play a mediatory role and are also often portrayed as politically subversive (Wilson 1995: 120-34). So even though the priestly and deuteronomic material suggests that eunuchs were marginalized in the ancient Israelite community they are nevertheless present in the biblical text. Isaiah looks forward to a time when eunuchs will no longer be cut off from the community but given 'a monument and a name better than sons and daughters' (Isa. 56.3-5). In the Acts of the Apostles an Ethiopian eunuch reading from the prophet Isaiah is baptized by Philip into the body of Christ (Acts 8.26-40). Early Christian theologians saw in the person and teaching of Jesus the dawn of the age that Isaiah had prophesied. And in Mt. 19.12 Jesus appears to site himself in a place equivalent to and in solidarity with the eunuch. If Kolakowski and Wilson are right that the disruption of the ordering of society in terms of reproduction is crucial to the gospel vision and that the disruption of other boundaries follows this—the boundaries of gender and identity ('foreigners' are mentioned with eunuchs in Isaiah's vision of inclusiveness)—then the transgendered

---

1.   The Hebrew word for eunuch, *saris*, can also refer to a government official which perhaps suggests that it was normal practice to castrate courtiers.

experience of embodiment must have a central place in the symposium of theological discourse on gender.

Flaunting It: The Body and Transgressive Practice

The body knowledge which propelled people like Comstock and May 'out' has also been experienced in corporate terms in the lesbian and gay community. The Stonewall Riots of June 1969 have achieved the status of myth as the moment when the modern gay liberation movement began. After Stonewall, it is often said, lesbian and gay people were no longer prepared to be defined by others, we became the subjects of our own history; we were no longer simply prepared to accept the normativity of heterosexuality and seek acceptance on the basis of conformity to its norms. Lesbian and gay people now felt they had something to teach the heterosexual world about love, bodiliness and relationships. In truth, this sea-change in lesbian and gay self-perception was emerging well before Stonewall, partly inspired by the feminist and black civil rights movements. But Stonewall became the historical moment at which a handful of people assented to this new self-perception in their bodies and acted upon it in a public manner, inspiring others to do the same. The people who took part in the original Stonewall Riots were not 'respectable' gay men and lesbians, they were drag queens, street hustlers, butch dykes who regularly had to suffer the indignity of police brutality, harassment and extortion. But on the night of 27 June 1969 the patrons of the Stonewall Inn in Greenwich Village, New York, did not just 'go quietly' when the police raided the establishment, they fought back and fought back for four nights. This is a clear example of Martin's contention that it is the people who are furthest away from the centre of the dominating power who are able to articulate and embody alternative understandings of reality.

What exploded at Stonewall was *anger*. Within the Christian tradition anger has been cast as a deadly sin but Beverly Harrison has noted that anger is an expression of deep bodily knowledge. It is a

> feeling-signal that all is not well in our relation to other persons or groups or to the world around us. Anger is a mode of connectedness to others and it is always a vivid form of caring. To put the point another way: anger is—and it always is—a sign of some resistance in ourselves to the moral quality of social relations in which we are immersed... Where anger rises, there the energy to act is present (Harrison 1990: 206).

Anger does not automatically inspire us to act correctly or justly. We have to reflect on what to do with our anger but anger plays a vital part in articulating the erotic, the yearning for connection and right relation with others. Harrison believes that the suppression of feeling as the basis of moral reflection leads to a disconnection with the world and therefore an impaired rationality and a tendency to act inhumanely.

What also exploded in the aftermath of Stonewall among lesbian and gay people around the world was pride. Indeed, every year the anniversary of the Stonewall Riots is commemorated with Pride marches and festivals. Pride, too, is a deep bodily feeling: we talk about our hearts bursting with pride, when we feel proud our posture often changes, we lift our heads. Pride, too, has often been designated as a sin in the Christian tradition. As with anger, pride does not necessarily lead to moral action but it is again a signal feeling of connection. For lesbian and gay people it is a deep bodily 'yes' to themselves and to others, and for Heyward it is a 'yes' to our craving for mutuality and justice.

Stonewall is an example of transgressive bodies engaging in transgressive action. Within the lesbian and gay liberation movements there have always been those who sought to integrate lesbian and gay people into pre-existing structures, whether of state or Church, and there have always been others ready to denounce such assimilationist practices on the grounds that the pre-existing structures, built upon and reflecting patriarchal and heterosexist norms and assumptions, can offer no real freedom. Transgressive lesbian and gay activists emphasize or 'flaunt' the difference between straight and gay, form alliances with all those marginalized by heterosexism (the term 'queer' was coined to describe this coalition) and *put their bodies* against violence and oppression through activities such as marches, sit-ins and so on. For some this has been literally a strategy for survival. Those living with HIV and AIDS, particularly in the USA, found that the only way effectively to challenge government indifference to the deaths of vast numbers of gay men and the exploitative practices of drug companies was to 'Act Up', taking to the streets and to the offices of institutions which otherwise ignored them. The gay theologian Robert Goss believes that transgressive activism is not merely an option for those who follow Christ but is essential to such discipleship. Jesus' announcement of the reign (*basileia*) of God was not merely a vision, it was a practice, an embodiment of a radical egalitarianism and subversion of dominant power matrixes. Jesus used his body in such a way as to disrupt the socio-politico-religious order, whether that was through touching the unclean, eating with the wicked, preventing the execution of a woman caught in adultery or turning over tables in the temple. For Goss, in the West, queer Christians are leading the way in a recovery of the power of prophetic action and embodied witness as an integral part of the proclamation of the *basileia* (Goss 1993). Goss also makes the point that queer communities have to practise the radical vision of the *basileia* within themselves, for an awareness of embodiment has often resulted in body fascism; a determination to reclaim the value of pleasure has often blinded people to the issues of racism, sexism and classism; a yearning for freedom has often been allowed to be uncritically manipulated and exploited by an economic system which associates freedom with ability to acquire and spend money and which hides the dehumanizing exploitation upon which it thrives (Goss 1993:156-59).

The Body and Friendship

Which model of relating embodies or has the potential to best embody the power of the erotic, the sacred yearning within us for right relationship? Several lesbian feminist writers, including Heyward (1989), Mary Hunt (1991) and Elizabeth Stuart (1995), have advanced the model of friendship. Friendship is employed for a number of reasons. It reflects the high value that women have traditionally placed upon friendship. It picks up the language that lesbian and gay people often use to speak about their most significant relationships. Friendship is a model of relating which has historically in the West been understood to have nothing to do with sexual desire and is therefore used to convey the fact that sexual desire is not only ordered towards or experienced in the genital area but is part of the erotic desire that permeates all our yearning for right relation. Friendship is also a mode of relating open to all, gay, straight, celibate, male, female, black, white, rich and poor, and it is a relationship which is based upon equality. Friendship has a long history of being valued in the Christian tradition—mostly in the context of celibate relationships (although Aquinas regarded marriage as a deep friendship[2])—and it can be argued that it was the model of relating embodied by Christ. Yet, from the sixteenth century onwards it was displaced by marriage which not only idolized and idealized male/ female relationships but constructed them in terms that made friendship

2.   *Summa Contra Gentiles* 3.2.123.6.

both within and outside marriage difficult. The model of friendship and the concept of *eros* to which it is often tied have recently been the subject of a great deal of critical analysis from gay men and from non-lesbian feminist women. From his perspective as a gay man Martin Stringer believes that the use of the model of friendship actually serves to marginalize sex, by diverting attention away from sexual acts. He also believes that the emphasis placed upon justice, mutuality and sacredness in the theologies of erotic power inevitably leads to the conclusion that sexual acts are appropriate only within quality relationships, as needing a high level of intimacy before they can be fully expressed or appreciated. This has the inevitable effect of placing the sexual act on such a high pedestal (as that which should always be sacred in and of itself) that we have to be extremely careful about the particular contexts in which we use it. Sex, it appears, is to be treated with caution, hidden away and isolated. This is not what such writers are actually aiming for, far from it, but this is the inevitable consequence of their language and their argument (Stringer 1997: 27-43). This emphasis on the quality of the relationship actually perpetuates the traditional Christian framework of good sex (in marriage) versus bad sex (all other sex) but in different terms. Stringer maintains that theologians have to learn from the 'second revolution' which took place in the 1980s (partly in response to the AIDS crisis) which has widened public understanding of sexuality and what constitutes a sexual act. This is evident, for example, in an increased awareness of sexual harassment and its multiple forms. Every part of the body and not just the genital region is potentially eroticized. But,

> It does not say that unless a person is having a whole body experience that person is not having sex. It says 'experiment', 'try out new things', 'eat ice-cream off your partner's flesh', 'look for the erogenous zones beyond the genital areas', 'explore the sense of touch, taste, smell within a sexual context', 'develop a sexual imagination' and, quite simply, 'enjoy yourselves in safe and uncomplicated fun' (Stringer 1997: 35).

This approach to sexuality is decidedly not dualistic, because the emphasis is on what we do with our bodies, not on internal or sacred powers or who we are. What matters is that the individual discovers through experiment what they find erotic and are open and honest about that with themselves and others. Stringer employs the metaphor of the meal to illustrate his approach,

Not all meals are 'sacred', although some intimate and romantic meals between very close friends may take this form. The presence of such meals does not, however, stop us sharing good meals with others, enjoying good wine, good food and good company. Within such context a certain sharing of each other's bodies should not be impossible, simply as an extension of the sharing which has been taking place within the meal. Sexual acts can be shared, like food, between friends and they can be enjoyed without guilt or hang ups (Stringer 1997: 41).

Karen Lebacqz finds difficulties with erotic theology for other reasons (Lebacqz 1994: 244-61). As a heterosexual woman she finds the language of 'intimacy', 'mutuality', 'reciprocity' and so on, language which assumes the equality of the partners involved, impossible to translate into a heterosexual setting precisely because men and women are not equal in terms of power or status and therefore any sexual ethic which seeks to be grounded in the lived experience of moral agents needs to centralise this imbalance of power. Lebacqz attempts to do this by reflecting as a woman on the injunction to love your enemy. She applies the term enemy to men to draw attention to the way in which the unequal distribution of power profoundly affects the relations between men and women. She draws first on the work of Martin Luther King Jr who placed forgiveness at the heart of the process of loving the enemy. Forgiveness for King was not about ignoring evil or bypassing repentance but resolving to act as if the past did not determine the future. It is a willingness, following recognition of wrong and repentance, to start afresh. Forgiveness recognizes that while someone is still the enemy that may not always have to be so. Then Lebacqz turns to another African-American theologian, Katie Cannon, who has argued that the lived experience of black women in the USA has been about survival, not the freedom of choice or consent which are the necessary for mutuality. The 'hard-nosed realism' which the imperative of survival induces should inform our sexual ethics according to Lebacqz, not a dream or vision of a society of equals which does not exist. Loving the enemy in terms of survival means seeking relationships with those 'enemies' who actively attempt to resist the culture of male domination. Lebacqz calls her ethic a 'role-based' ethic for it acknowledges that all our relationships take place in a culturally conditioned context which to some extent dictates how we relate to one another. The language of erotic theology offers no help to heterosexual women facing the complexities of loving the enemy.

Linda Woodhead takes issue with erotic theology and would also take issue with Stringer's approach on the grounds that both are grounded in and help maintain a thoroughly privatized and individualistic understanding of embodiment, sexuality and sex. Not only is 'sexuality' now understood primarily as a matter of an individual's identity but sex too is privatized and individualized by the emphasis on pleasure and satisfaction. Woodhead would find Stringer's emphasis upon pleasure and freedom (within boundaries of consent) a classic liberal, utilitarian approach: 'sex's sole *telos* becomes the pleasure of the free individual' and therefore ultimately all sexual acts are masturbatory (Woodhead 1997: 101). Woodhead also finds little to commend in the distinctive approach of 'body theology' as it has been developed by theologians such as James Nelson. Usually centralized in the doctrine of the incarnation,

> the meaning of the incarnation is here squeezed and reduced until it comes to speak only of the importance of the bodily nature of the individual and loses connection with Jesus Christ. The exhortation to take an incarnational perspective comes to mean that one should rely on one's own individual experience in sexual reflection rather than that one should bring such reflection under the authority of God's revelation in Christ (Woodhead 1997: 103).

Thus, beneath the theological language lies a barely hidden privatized and individualistic approach to the body. Woodhead acknowledges that the deployment of the concept of *eros* by feminist theologians is an attempt to move beyond an individualistic and privatized understanding of sexuality by naming it as a power which pushes us toward right relationship in every aspect of our lives and which seeks ultimately to connect all things in right relation. Yet Woodhead is still suspicious of *eros* theology because she fears that in practice it ends up grounding the power of eros in the individual sexual experience, thus ignoring Foucault's central point which was that erotic experience is mediated through various matrixes of power as well as influencing them. The Christian tradition, she claims, long ago grasped this fact and therefore focused its attention upon the transforming of these institutions so that good experience could flow from them.

> On a Christian understanding, the entrance into true relationship with God and neighbour is made possible only by entrance into the church, the new community called into being by God. It is the body of Christ which forms the basis of a new society—not the body of the individual (Woodhead 1997: 106).

Woodhead agrees with exponents of *eros* theology that sex does seem to be constantly pushing one beyond an autonomous individualism, even masturbation generally involves the imaginary presence of an other, however objectified. But sex also pushes out beyond the boundaries of two through the recrystallization of networks of relationships that occur when people become couples and through the procreation of children. Marriage as a public ritual both acknowledges the public dimension to sexual relationships and constitutes that relationships in relation to 'God, friends, family, church, and state' (Woodhead 1997: 109). Woodhead argues that for Christians the primary context in which sex takes place is in the body of Christ. Early Christian writers developed a theology of relationship out of their experience of God not vice versa and of their being first and foremost part of a new community. This led to two broad approaches to sexual relationships: either they were regarded as an unnecessary distraction from the prior and more important relationships of God and community or, in so far as such relationships mirror the relationship between Christ and the Church, they are good and holy. What our ancestors in faith therefore remind us today is that sex is both not as important as and is more important than contemporary western society acknowledges. In a society which tends to collapse personhood into sexuality and coupledom, thus marginalizing huge numbers of men and women, our foreparents remind us that our primary relationships by which we are constituted as persons are with God and our neighbour. On the other hand, in a society which values sexual activity primarily in terms of personal pleasure, we are reminded that sexual activity has a profound, ripple effect upon the network of relations in which the activity is conducted. And so *eros* theology and the theology of friendship which so often accompanies it are beset on all sides. Stringer accuses them of marginalizing sex and Woodhead of ultimately collapsing all relational energy, including the divine, into the individual's experience of pleasure. Lebacqz accuses them of being hopelessly unrealistic, at least if applied to heterosexual relationships.

To deal with Lebacqz's point first, it is quite wrong to characterize erotic theology as assuming or demanding that mutuality, equality, friendship exist prior to a relationship. All the theologians who have articulated this type of theology have taken very seriously the fact that we are formed as persons and in relationships in a context of non-mutuality, non-equality, in a context which does not value friendship.

Friendship is something we have to learn and work towards, building
upon snatches of experience and visions which have been handed down
to us and which we ourselves create. The erotic power is a power of
'yearning', of possibility. However, it may be true that eros theology has
failed to reflect on realistic theo-ethical strategies for working out that
yearning in the middle of hetero-patriarchal reality.

Woodhead, on the other hand, completely ignores hetero-patriarchal
reality in her use of biblical texts and in her centralizing of marriage. She
leaves unexamined the construction of both the relationship of Christ to
his Church and husband to wife in terms of slavery. She gives no indi-
cation of where her centralizing of marriage leaves lesbian and gay
people and shows no awareness of how the social prioritizing of marriage has impacted on them. She also fails to note that, despite the public ritualization of marriage, it is in fact one of the most privatized
relationships, open to no scrutiny whatsoever. The Church shows even
less interest than the state in domestic violence, marital rape, and plain
misery in marriage. Similarly the organization of the modern nuclear
family in the West appears to collapse relationality and community into
a very narrow circle indeed. Lesbian feminist theologians endeavour to
respond to this reality. There is no dualism in their theology between
'tradition' and 'experience'. Tradition consists of the reflected experience of our ancestors in faith which in turn both forms us and demands
that we continue the process in the humble (but biblical) belief that the
Spirit is still among us revealing more truth. God is never reduced to
individual experience, never mind sexual experience, but may be
encountered there. The theological context for speaking about sex and
embodiment in erotic theology is the body of Christ(a) but it is a body
set against the maginalizing, violent and exclusionary practices of
hetero-patriarchy and this resistance is itself inspired by resistance in the
biblical text and tradition. Woodhead's reflection on the tradition leads
her to state strongly that sexuality must be unitive and therefore must
take place within a life-long committed relationship. However, Kathy
Rudy has suggested that perhaps one of the best examples of unitive sex
which takes place in the context of community is the communal sex
practised by gay men in large cities, each sexual encounter reinforcing a
sense of identity and belonging, 'and although no two members of the
community make steadfast promises to any one person in the community, each in his own way promises himself as part of this world. Intimacy and faithfulness in sex are played out on the community rather

than individual level' (Rudy 1996: 90). Such sex is also procreative in the sense that it creates new life, the community is enlarged and enriched. Rudy does not want to romanticize the practice of communal sex, she knows that it can take place within a context of 'lying, cheating and adultery', as well as violence, but just as not all monogamous sex is unitive nor is all communal sex exploitative. Gay men may be the people to teach Christians how to be part of a community wider than the nuclear family. Woodhead's theological method, grounded uncritically in certain biblical texts and traditions, would simply not leave her any space to offer a serious consideration of this gay experience.

Yet Rudy's experience of identifying as a lesbian has caused her to question the interpretation of tradition offered by people like Woodhead. Rudy maintains that such theologians read back into the biblical tradition a centralizing of heterosexuality, marriage and family life which reflects not the biblical tradition itself but the construction of western (and particularly American) industrial society, which banished women to the private sphere and placed upon them the burden of being the family's point of contact with the divine. Christianity along with women was thoroughly domesticated and the association of Christian orthodoxy with clear differentiated gender roles and the shrinking family unit was established. Rudy therefore understands Christian fundamentalists' fear and loathing of feminism and lesbian and gay liberation to be rooted in a fear of losing contact with a God who is known through gender or rather a particular construction of it (Rudy 1997: 15-66). Rudy draws attention to the fact that in the fundamentalists' discourse but also in most other contemporary Christian discourse the family has replaced the Church as a Christian's primary social commitment, with even lesbian and gay theologians and their supporters arguing for the acceptance and blessing of non-heterosexual relationships on the basis that they resemble the modern heterosexual nuclear family. Rudy notes that this displacement of the Church by the family has absolutely no basis in the Christian tradition and is indeed antithetical to it. But Rudy goes even further than this, drawing upon the work of queer theory (Butler: 1990) which has highlighted the way in which categories of bodily identity (such as sexuality and gender) are produced and performed within a specific and historically and socially constructed symbolic system. She is insistent that for Christians their primary bodily identification should be 'Christian'. This has profound repercussions because a person becomes a Christian not through biology but through baptism—issues of biology and gender should therefore be of no concern to Christian communities, in the sense that whether people are male, female or transgendered, gay, lesbian or bisexual should have no significance in the way in which the Christian community organizes itself and scrutinizes its own members and society as a whole. Any sexual ethic (or indeed any ethic) must begin in the baptismal experience of being called into a unitive relationship with the whole of God's people. Rudy thus manages to avoid the individualism that some have accused exponents of erotic theology of failing to avoid, while also taking queer experience seriously. She too is critical of erotic theology and particularly the quest for mutuality in sexual relationships that is at its heart. Rudy finds such a quest unrealistic, believing that it is impossible to expel issues of power and the cultural construction of desire from relationships. Rather:

> What the church today needs is a way to recapture the intentions behind the early formulas of sexual ethics. Unitivity and procreativity in their earliest articulations were designed to make a public statement concerning sexuality within the Christian community. Sex for Christians would be something that not only drew the people involved in the act closer together; it would also draw them closer to God and closer to the entire worshipping community (Rudy 1997: 125).

For Rudy as for an increasing number of lesbian and gay theologians, what Scripture teaches us is that 'what is ultimately pleasing to God about our sexuality is hospitality. If our sexual relations help us to open our hearts and homes to lost travellers and needy strangers, they are good. And if they cause us to be aggressively territorial and abusive to outsiders, they are evil' (Rudy 1997: 126). Rudy's approach resonates with the work of a number of post-modern theologians who draw attention to the subversive parodying of gender that takes place in early Christian theology in its attempt to express the relationship between Christ, the Church and God. As Gerard Loughlin notes,

> The unified difference of Christ and church is variously parodied: as head and members of one body, as the nuptial embrace of bridegroom and bride, and of mother and child. Here it is Mary who attains to the pitch of parodic substitution, since she is both the mother of Jesus and, as mother-church, of each member of his body; but as the church she is also the bride of Christ, not only the mother but the wife of her son. (Here we are reminded that what I have called parodic substitution allows Christianity to place at its symbolic centre certain cultural taboos—against cannibalism, incest and homosexuality—and break them.) (Loughlin: 1998: 13)

In Eph. 5.21-27 the male Christ is portrayed as having a female body in terms of the Church. The language used to formulate and develop the concept of the Trinity is equally queer, the father begets the son with whom and with the spirit he engages in a never ending exchange of love and mutual self-donation.

> In this way, what out culture may dictate as our sex and gender, will no longer be determinative of our freedom to give and receive love. For truly in Christ there is no male and female, only the reciprocation of bodies; beautiful parodies of the trinitarian donation (Loughlin 1998: 21).

If the Church were to adopt Rudy's two criteria for judging the morality of sexual relationships—unitivity and hospitality—the contemporary construction and sacralizing of heterosexual marriage would come under some much needed critical scrutiny and matters of sexuality would be kept in the public, communal domain. It is certainly hard to understand how Stringer's emphasis on the priority of individual desire fits into a Christian vision at all and perhaps the absence of any theological reflection in the article examined may suggest that it does not and that the second sexual revolution actually pushes us beyond Christianity altogether (Stringer 1996: 15). Ironically, even though he finds so little merit in the model of friendship, it is this model he uses in the context of a meal to illustrate his point about various forms of sexual practice. There are other questions we might ask of queer theology and the body. For example, does it simply end up essentializing the body and friendship? But we are witnessing a community taking the body very seriously and wrestling within itself as to the theological meaning and implications of embodiment. The honesty as well as the passion of the debate has a great deal to teach the Churches.

Chapter Six

The Body and the World

An incarnational religion that declares universal salvation must pay attention to all that is incarnate. In other words, to the whole of the created order and the very fibres of the universe itself. If we are no longer thinking in purely individualistic terms of salvation for 'my soul', then we have to rethink our concept of redemption. Further, if the lived experience of women and men is the stuff where this redemption occurs it would seem necessary to have a world in which to live and breathe. Unfortunately this has not always been the way in which Christianity has seen things. The reasons for this are complex but possibly begin with the Christian interpretation of the Genesis story which has set the trend for body and world negating theology. It seems crucial to acknowledge the Babylonian background to the story as well as the philosophical cosmology of Plato that has been so often used by Christians when interpreting it if we are to escape this negativity.

Snakes and Scientists: The Story so Far!

As it stands the Eden myth tells us that the disembodied word of God commanded that the world be brought into being out of nothingness with a hierarchy of creation set in place ending with humans (Gen. 1.27), man (Gen. 2.7) or woman (Gen. 2.22). As the crown of creation the humans are given the task of subduing (Hb, *kabas* = stamp down) and dominating (Hb, *rada* = trampling) the world (Gen. 1.28) which is signalled by the power of naming (Gen. 2.19). While man is busy 'naming and subduing' the woman is busy exploring and gaining 'hands on' experience of their environment. She communes with other parts of the created order, seeing them as equal and wishes to gain as much knowledge as possible. For her 'sins' we are told the Fall of Man

occurred. While we are aware that our eyes on this story render a rather
different interpretation we use this simply to illustrate the point that
interpretation is all. After all there are Gnostic texts that see the Eden
event in a very different light. They interpret the actions of Eve as spiritually motivated and the injunction not to eat as springing from jealousy
and small mindedness on behalf of the lesser gods. The 'punishment'
that the pair received was again vindictive and designed to ensure that
amid the toil and despair they would now endure they would have no
time to contemplate spiritual matters. The story, therefore, shows how
those who feel they have spiritual understanding wish to claim it for
themselves and will bar the way of others, even by inflicting punishment
on them (*The Hypostasis of the Archons* 88.12-91.12).

There is an increasing body of work (Westermann 1974; Long 1991;
Stone 1982) which suggests that the Genesis story is male polemic
against a much older and more ecologically sound goddess culture. The
Babylonian texts which form the background for the Genesis myth are
more honest in stating their intentions. They clearly illustrate how the
mother goddess is challenged and defeated. The Genesis myth does not
declare its intention so openly but all the signs are there. All that was
valued and honoured in the goddess culture is cast down and made suspect at best, or the root of all evil at worst. In the patriarchal myth,
women, nature, the wise serpent and the procreative process itself are
seen as suspect.

While there is no time to go into the intricate details of the argument
for goddess culture it is useful to illustrate that the texts as we have them
are not straightforward accounts of how people saw things. They have a
background and a purpose, they are patriarchal propaganda and as such
should be treated with caution. The Jewish tradition, while using the
same texts, has not suffered from the same degree of body and world
negative interpretations. This is largely due to the fact that they do not
employ Platonic thought with its implicit dualism to interpret them.
Reading the story with Platonic eyes encourages the reader to remove
himself as far as possible from nature and women who are nearer to the
created order and its evil. This at least was the conclusion of Augustine
and many other notables who came after him. For them the Genesis
story clearly shows how both women and nature need to be subdued if
they are not to break out into chaotic and world destroying activity. It is
the task of the more rational, that is more disconnected from the created
order, male to ensure that both women and the world know their place

in the business of his salvation. Man is entitled to use both nature and woman for his needs but he must never get too close to either and must always remember that he has the power of naming, he is their master.

Religion and its mythology have a deep hold on people's psyches and we cannot afford to hope that these stories will simply be ignored. Symbols do not rely on rational assent and so we have to be extremely careful with the symbolic world that we portray. The Genesis myth sets in place a hierarchy that must ultimately cause destruction. It would be unwise to suggest that a return to goddess worship would immediately solve our ecological problems. However, it is useful to contrast ways of seeing the world and the praxis these views generate. It has been argued that the divine female can be traced back to the Upper Paleolithic cultures of 25,000 BCE encouraged relation with the earth since the goddess herself was understood as being the earth. The way to wisdom then lay in close connection with creation that was based on mutuality and not colonization of the fruits of the earth. Many contemporary goddess worshippers claim that they are striking at the heart of estrangement that patriarchal theology has introduced into the world by proclaiming value in the bodies of women and in the created order itself. For many following the goddess is about choosing a way to life rather than belief, it is about sacredness in the stuff of life. It is also about taking responsibility and not assuming that an outside agency will intervene when the mess we make becomes too great. If we pollute the world it will return the compliment and the faithful will not be placed in small oxygen chambers before being whisked off to heaven! The emphasis on this world being the reality and not a prelude for some other, better existence is a very positive contribution to the ecological debate. The question remains whether or not the Christian tradition has sufficient resources to view the world as the body of God or whether it has to continue its armed hostility to the created order.

At first glance a religion that glories in sacrifice and eagerly awaits the end of time is hardly an inspiring place to find a positive eco-theology. The doctrines of traditional Christian theology read more like cosmic sado-masochism than empowered mutual relation. Perhaps the answer lies in the hands of the scientists, they may be able to free us from the tyranny of mythology. Unfortunately, this has not proved to be the case. It was a misplaced hope that the scientific revolution could overcome the destructive dualisms of patriarchal mythology. In fact the picture became worse. Darwinian insights reduced the status of nature still further with humans so far up the evolutionary tree that they could no longer see the anguish of mother earth. Creation, it was strongly argued was there to serve the higher evolutionary needs, those of man. Darwin and Newton both removed the 'soul' from nature and left it as nothing more than lifeless particles of dead matter. Nature became even more objectified.

Newton retained the notion of a deity but one that was even more removed from creation than before. This deity set the world in motion and then withdrew to let it tick on according to set patterns and mechanical processes. Scientists who held this opinion therefore felt free to dismember the world in order to reveal its inner workings and dominate it completely. Francis Bacon expressed most eloquently the dominance philosophy:

> The new man of science must not think that the 'inquisition of nature is in any way interdicted or forbidden'. Nature must be 'bound into service' and made a slave, put in constraint and molded by the mechanical arts (Merchant 1980: 8-9).

His desire to exert such power over the created order had a religious dimension as he wanted to gain back the control that had been lost through the actions of Eve (Halkes 1991: 57). Like the victim of rape the created order had no face, no soul and was in the power of external forces to be abused at will.

As the scientific model took hold the notion of God was gradually discarded and the scientist was set in the place of the external all-knowing, all-powerful deity. The iron grip of the patriarch continued but this time he was located in the laboratory and not heaven. Nothing is seen as left to chance and nature is still believed to be in chains to omniscient power. Religious mythology has been replaced by scientific mythology and both are dangerous and abusive of nature and humans. Christ will no longer 'fix' things at the end of time, he will not need to as the scientists will ensure there is no end of time. This attitude is well illustrated by Nobel Prize winner, Robert Solow, who assured us in 1987:

> The world in effect can get along without natural resources, so exhaustion is just an event, not a catastrophe (Gnanadson in Ruether 1996: 77).

What is even more shocking is that this view was not challenged in any serious way. The scientific mythology, like the religious before it, is blind in the face of evidence. The new gods were powerless to move the Chenobyl cloud even one inch yet their confidence in their own omnipotence remains unshaken. Science has not rescued us from the unreality of religious mythology it has simply hijacked the power attached to myth.

We are facing global crisis not because the earth is dysfunctional and is no longer able to sustain itself but because of the way in which humans approach it and the demands we make of it. This means that we have to accept responsibility for change rather than project inadequacies on to the earth. The reason that this is not best left to scientists alone is that the way in which we approach the earth is not a 'purely scientific' area. That is to say that science is not a 'pure' activity it is as affected by culture as any other discipline. It is, therefore, according to Vandana Shiva, not a value free and objective discipline but a 'Western, bour- geois, masculine project' (in Ruether 1996: 67). It is then an area that should be critiqued by feminist liberation theology. This critique is based on giving voice to the marginalized and oppressed which in this case means many in the Third World who daily face the consequence of western disregard of their needs as well as the earth itself which is so cruelly abused.

It is often thought that the needs of those in the Third World are served through development programmmes. However, the work of Shiva and others clearly shows that this is yet another advanced capitalist myth that serves the developed world more than the 'developing world'. While development programmes have created new forms of affluence they have done so at great expense to the already dispossessed. Focusing on the plight of women Shiva shows how development has become the problem it was attempting to alleviate. Economic growth has become a new form of colonialism which drains the resources of those who are most in need of them. For example, the expansion of cash crops has actually dispossessed women even further as it has removed them from a means of production, that of growing food, and has left them with fewer resources to fed their children. Cash cropping destroys the soil and the water and therefore prevents the renewal of the resources (Shiva in Ruether 1996: 65).

Shiva makes the point that there is now a crisis of survival brought about by development programmes which are patriarchal projects springing from western capitalism. These projects do not fit well with another way of life nor do they respect the difference. Productivity for survival is a very different matter than productivity to satisfy the capi- talist market. Most women in India are poor and they work daily in the production of survival yet, 'women and nature working to produce and reproduce life are declared "unproductive"' (Shiva in Ruether 1996: 67). When control and profit take the upper hand women and nature become linked in a downward spiral. There is nothing new in saying that women and nature are linked. Indeed, there could be dangers in speaking of any kind of special relationship between women and mother earth. It can lead to either a demeaning of women or to romantic, self-indulgent and unrealistic notions about the special nature of women. Shiva makes neither of these mistakes, she declares that the revolution lies in maintaining that the connection between women and the earth has always been in order to enhance life both of people and the earth itself. It is therefore important that this connection should be given more respect. She counsels strongly against the control ethic seeing it as leading to ultimate lack of control. Eventually we will not be able to control nature but more worryingly our interventions in nature will mean that it also loses control of itself.

Although women are themselves victims of the degeneration of the environment they are also active in movements to protect it from the onslaughts of 'development'. Many have developed their own coopera-tives in the hope of opting out of mainline development programmes. Although the women become more disempowered by the development programmes they are still expected to provide for their children by finding fuel and water. Even though there are always children there are not always resources. Women are therefore held hostage to their families and to survival (Gnanadson in Hallman 1993: 183).

The different approaches of women and development agencies and those wishing to bring 'people into the 20th century' is highlighted in a confrontation between the Chipko movement (an Indian movement of women to save forests) and foresters. The foresters told the women that the trees were resin and timber, that is profit, while the women sang songs about the forest being soil, water and pure air. They reminded the foresters that if the earth is sutained she will sustain us (Shiva 1986: 5). There are two languages being spoken here, one of profit and one of care. The reality of Babel.

It would appear that the needs of people and the planet are not met through development programmes and the control ethic of capitalist production. A liberation theology based on embodied empowerment has to begin elsewhere! Further, we need to be aware that in placing the needs of the planet first we are challenging global capitalism at its heart.

This is a system that has abused women, men and nature in its relentless pursuit of obscenely large profit margins. This is not an uncritical Marxist critique of the capitalist order but rather a suggestion that capital for its own sake has brought us to the point of extinction. It seems that modes of production should be both person and planet friendly and that capital should serve all people rather than just a few while the rest are faceless servants of its production. (Witness the way in which Tower Colliery closed by the Coal Board for being unproductive has been turned around by the miners who bought it. Their priority was not profit but the maintenance of jobs. They are making enough profit to increase jobs and make the working life of all much better.) This is not an argument for a return to some unspoiled paradise or to raising goats and growing vegetables in Surbiton. Rather a plea for a more harmonious existence with nature, a sustainable approach where the needs of the planet are paramount. This in turn means that we have to listen to others about the way in which their part of the planet thrives rather than approach the world with a master plan geared towards profit. Ruether illustrates the point well with her story of strawberries:

> I remember standing in a market in January looking greedily at boxes of beautiful strawberries and wondering if I might be able to sneak some back through customs into the United States to my snow-covered home. A friend...said softly 'Beautiful aren't they?...and they are covered with blood' (1996: 5).

Those strawberries were tended by people who barely had enough to buy bread and who suffered from pesticide-induced illnesses that brought premature death. How badly do we in the West want to eat fruits and vegetables that are out of our season? Ruether urges dialogue with women from Africa, Asia and Latin America as this bases the reality of impoverishment of land and people in a context and not just in dry theory. We are part of the 20 per cent who use 82 per cent of the world's resources and it will benefit no one if we decide to be in the bottom 18 per cent. What is needed is that we listen and transform our systems culturally and economically (Ruether 1996: 8).

Models of Liberation

Mary Hunt begins her liberation ecology by seeing it as an extension of the mutual and ethical friendship that we strive for with humans. The strength of this approach is that in extending 'friendship' to others we will at some point have to realize that this requires a transformative approach to the earth itself. If we are striving for mutuality with Asian or African women we will, sooner or later, realize that many of our economic policies have dire consequences for them and their children. However, Hunt's view does not seem to value the earth for its own sake but only in relation to its ability to sustain human life. While this is important an ecotheology that places value on the earth for its own sake, one that moves away from androcentric thinking would probably be better.

Anne Primavesi makes a step in this direction by encouraging us to relate to things as though they were sacred in themselves and notes that hierarchy is not the only way to ensure against anarchy (1991: 151). Her alternative is that of ecological community. This is a concept fuelled by the notions of both the cosmic Christ and process thought. The cosmic Christ highlights the reality that unless all the created order is saved then nothing can be. The salvific nature of the Christ had to animate the whole universe. This places ecology right at the centre of Christian concerns and not as a marginal question to get round to when the important business of individual salvation has been dealt with. No such division can be made 'all creation is simultaneously being loved and created by God or else none of it is' (Primavesi 1991: 151). How differently we have to view the world if we take her seriously, she is no longer just a commodity. By placing Christ in the world in this way we are able to look around and not just upwards in order to see the mystery present in all creation. Primavesi argues that seeing Christ in creation cannot just remain at the mystical level but has to lead to political action. Contemplating the suffering Christ in a world that is drowning in its own waste is not what is required of a Christian, being committed to policies and praxis that clear up the waste is what is required.

Primavesi outlines how traditional Christology has created a lack of ecological awareness. By placing Christ outside the created order and theologizing about heaven and the end of time Christians have often set their face to fleeing the earth rather than engaging with it. By focusing on the cosmic Christ a very welcome change in emphasis is introduced to the debate. However, why are Christians unable to value the world in itself and why does it somehow have to be seen as working with us towards a larger androcentric plan. Halkes openly acknowledges that the created order has its own value system that is not in any way related to ours and may not even be in our interests (1991: 93). This she claims is still a Christian position. This view seems wholly consistent with a feminist acceptance of difference and diversity. The earth may indeed have its own value system and is quite able to exist without us and not in our interests and yet still be enlivened by that which we call the divine. Matthew Fox grants the world its own decision making powers but suggests that it conspired for our existence, we are gifts of the universe (1987: 10). In a concrete sense Fox is right, after all we would not be here if the conditions had not been right. However, the notion that we were in some way willed plays back into the destructive superiority that ecotheology should be keen to avoid. Surely it is time for cooperation with the cosmos based on its own integrity rather than our patriarchal value system and the innate destructiveness of androcentric thinking. It seems time to give up our desire for control and expand our vision.

The dominance we have exerted over nature in the name of divine election has been ecologically devastating and so it is time for a metanoia. Jay McDaniel reminds us that God created the world and saw it was good, as it is, not by adding goodness to it. He says:

> After creating animals on the fifth day God did not assign them goodness, God sees that they are good [Gen. 1.21]. God is God because she invites others to share her wisdom. She beckons us, humans made in her image, to recognise the intrinsic value that she herself sees (1989: 68).

McDaniel notes that with the increase in animal life there is a greater risk on the part of God since suffering will increase and God will appear to have less ability to harmonize creation. Therefore, he insists, a doctrine of continuous creativity needs to be linked with one of redemption or co-redemption (1989: 45). It seems that we youngsters on the planet have not really understood our mother's ways and her advice. Instead of working with her and valuing all as good we are the most destructive. There are five to ten million species on the planet but we will lose at least a third and possibly half if we do not change our ways.

McDaniel's work is stimulating and it would be interesting to extend his notion of co-creativity and co-redemption beyond the human realm. Could it be argued that nature herself is involved in the business of redeeming the planet by making it increasingly difficult for us to survive! We are after all the biggest offenders in the ecological process. If eco-theology is arguing for divine goodness and energy existing in all of creation and for this drive to be towards the setting in place of the fullness of God why does it have to include humans? Is this perhaps the last aspect of arrogant androcentrism? We are the youngest on the planet and the least well integrated, it is perhaps time that we became more humble and stood in awe of nature and her ways or left the picture altogether.

This is not to suggest that nature is co-creative or co-redemptive in a benign way. Indeed, the Christian God was not either, traditional views of redemption rest on the torture and death of a beloved son. Why then if we speak of our own extinction as being redemptive for the rest of creation does this seem a strange idea? McDaniel poses the problem of the white pelicans who lay two eggs, the second two days after the first. This later chick is purely a back-up in case the first is not strong. Should the first survive the second is sacrificed (1989: 19). This process has enabled the white pelicans to survive for thirty million years—therefore we have to conclude it is a successful strategy although worrying from the position of the second chick. This serves to highlight just how ambiguous co-creativity and co-redemption appear to be. The pelicans are thriving yet millions have been sacrificed over the centuries. If we intervened on behalf of the second chick we would undoubtedly in the long run bring about the extinction of all pelicans. Could it be that if we constantly intervene on our own behalf we will bring about total destruction of the planet, just as the second chick would devastate the pelicans if it lived. Sacrifice is called for and it is not so shocking to think that it may be humans who have to pay the ultimate price for the preservation of the planet.

Although McDaniel does not say so it appears that he is an evolutionist and so when he speaks of God sharing her wisdom and creating in her image he is referring to all the created order. We are merely a part of divine diversity not the pinnacle of creation and so why our extinction should concern us more than that of chimpanzees, who share 98 per cent of our genetic make-up, can only be put down to self-absorption. Can we with conscience make simple choices between people and nature—for example, knowing what we do, is it an easy choice between the destruction of an acre of rain forest or the lives of a dozen people living in some major city? Is it only false isolationism and tribalism that makes our guts react in favour of the people? As we have said these are not easy questions now that humans are seeking ecological justice, are no longer at the top of the tree and acknowledge the world as co-redemptive.

However, far from advocating mass suicide as the most ethical path for humans it is crucial that we find a mature way forward—one in which humans understand their place in nature and therefore can act co-creatively and co-redeemingly. McFague (1993) advocates a body-based approach—she feels that we should see trees and planets as bodies. This will enable us to connect in an intimate way with the world. It could open the way to overcoming the subject/object dualism that has enabled us to exploit the world. Barbara McClintock encourages us to feel for the organism (McDaniel 1989: 88) which will draw us into intimate connection. This feeling could be equated with the way in which God feels in creation where what is created is not outside the creator; there is no subject/object division. This will mean that we stop seeing ourselves as spirits in a material world and instead understand that we are spirited bodies amongst spirited bodies (McFague 1993: 19).

McFague places the emphasis on matter, bodies, because of her understanding of the way the universe itself evolved and functions. It took one very hot piece of matter approximately one millionth of a gram in weight to spawn billions of galaxies, planets and stars. (The first three minutes of creation being the busiest in fifteen billion years.) For McFague this underpins both the sameness and the diversity of the created order. She also believes that this highlights a reverse hierarchy in which the most complex creations on the planet are in fact dependent for their continued survival on the lowest forms. It was therefore very bad advice to encourage humans to subdue and dominate creation. Matter then is privileged in a way that Christianity has found hard to sustain, without it nothing else could exist, even mind (McFague 1993: 42). Further, when we view the world from the body we are situating ourselves in reality, not that this is the whole of reality, but McFague believes it more real than the utopian dreams of much Christian spirituality. She would not have us give up our dreams but simply engage in a more realistic way with the world as it is and not as it may be (1993: 71).

She suggests that we should see the world and God as a continuum and therefore act towards both in the same way. While McFague argues that all exist on a continuum she is also able to say that each living thing is both the *imago dei* and a subject in itself in radical interconnection with all other subjects (1997: 2-3). Therefore she encourages Christians to know the world and not flee from it. This knowledge is in both a big and a small way. The 'big way' takes on the scientific questions and answers and comes to see the world as structured yet open, enduring and novel. The 'small way' assumes the big way and then focuses on the neighbour be that a tree, a person or a frog (1997: 20-22). In order to come to love the world as we should we have to give it this kind of attention as we do not love what we do not know.

McFague is not arguing for a kind of mystical union with the world. Indeed she sees this as just another way of exploiting it. It is exploitation as we are using the world to back up our feelings rather than seeing as it is and for itself. We are told to 'consider the lillies of the field', which McFague understands as seeing the world as it is and respecting the differences. Of course seeing is not as easy as it sounds since we are all preconditioned in our seeing. To a greater or lesser extent we see what we expect to see. Our culture, affected as it is by its Christian heritage, has given us very androcentric, myopic vision. McFague is aware of the problems with vision and distinquishes between two types of seeing: with the arrogant eye and with the loving eye.

The arrogant eye sees everything in relation to itself and how all may serve it. To this end it simplifies everything since by denying complexity and mystery it is more able to turn others to its own needs. The loving eye on the other hand pays attention to the complexity and diversity in life and sees things quite apart from its own needs and fears (McFague 1997: 34). The loving eye is also more earth bound in the sense that it sees things as they really are without the interference of the distorting self-focused mind. It sees things in their context and therefore allows them status as subjects. This is not the same as fusing with nature as it requires much more attention to detail and embracing of diversity. McFague asserts that there are many subjects in the universe and there is no difference between them.

This may seem a totally revolutionary idea but in fact it is only in recent times that people have viewed nature as an object. During the mediaeval period nature was seen as instructing humans about the ways of God. It was contemplated for the clues it could give to the nature of God and the moral life. It was not seen as mechanistic but as alive with all that was necessary to lead us to a higher understanding. While this is a better attitude to nature than we have today it was unusual for nature to be valued in itself. In fact while nature may have been lauded in theory it was often demeaned in reality. Despite this the mediaeval period gave people a greater sense of identity with nature as well as a sense of belonging. It is very curious that science fiction is now so popular, is this to fill the gap opened up by our sense of isolation from nature? Do we really need someone out there because we can no longer acknowledge the living 'subjectness' of the earth on which we exist?

Embodied Ecology

McFague is suggesting touch as the radical solution to the ecological crisis. She points out that touch gives us both limits and a sense of inter-relationality. It also compels us to face difference and not get lost in 'oceanic feelings of oneness' which can numb us to the real question posed by the world (1997: 98). McFague insists that God is found in the depth and detail of life and does not exist despite the way the world is. She says:

> A model of being and knowing that begins with touch…will insist on being bonded to skin, fur, feathers, to the smells of the earth, to the intricate and detailed differences in people and other life forms (1997: 102).

This relational self/world model is according to McFague a sign of Christian maturity as there is a refusal to retreat from the world or to fuse with it. This model assumes multiple relationships with human and non-human life forms and understands that our experience shapes us. Unlike other feminist theologians McFague is against the notion of fantasy which she thinks distances us from the reality of people. We merely imagine how they may feel and do not take the time to actually look. She advocates perception based on touch. Her reservations about imagination and fantasy are understandable but people have found tremendous power in 'daring to imagine'. That is they see clearly the way the world is and actually allowing the power within themselves to go further, to know in the depth of themselves that another way is possible, one that at present can only be dreamt. This is surely the way in which great reforms and social movements have started; someone with vision has dared to imagine the impossible and has then worked like hell to bring it to reality. Remaining in the realm of fantasy is not a good thing but to give up on imagination would be a tragedy. After all if we are now going to have a commandment that reads 'do unto others as they would have you do to them' there has to be room for imagining how the other feels or how to best provide what it is they require. This of course is inter-relational imagination, people imagining together how the world may be and how to creatively move to the right balance.

Robert Pyle acknowledges the complex issues involved in the eco-logical crisis but is of the opinion that there is one central reason 'the extinction of experience of the earth' (McFague 1997: 115). People are no longer having close encounters with the earth that surrounds us. This raises all kinds of ethical questions in relation to town planning as well as environmental protection. It was found that during the LA riots in 1992 young people could easily identify automatic weapons by their sound. As McFague notes, 'the interior landscape is influenced by the exterior' (1997: 123). What this seems to suggest is that we need more authentic grounding on the planet if we are to develop as people who can once more feel for it and each other. Eco-theology then is beginning to enquire about the urban surroundings of people and not just about the rain forest. The living spaces provided for people will not only have an environmental impact in themselves but will encourage or discourage experiences of the earth. McFague highlights the fact that there are towns and cities that give people good experiences of the earth and emphasizes that she is not looking for a return to the wilderness. We have to create the kingdom around us but this can be in a garden as much as in the wild (1997: 160).

We can create these 'gardens' by working towards communities that have high levels of literacy and health care and low environmental impact. McFague rightly points out that such communities already exist, Kerala in Southern India being one such community where although the income cannot rival that of the USA their standard of living is high. In other words they are a fine example of low level economy, low environmental impact and a high quality of life. It could be said that they are living lightly on the planet. It is interesting, although it is not a point that McFague picks up, that Kerala was one of the regions in India that was matrifocal. Are women's ways of sitting on the planet still coming through in this culture and having a positive influence?

While McFague suggests that we go along the path of radical touch, Ruether suggests a conversion in thinking. It is her contention that we have to overcome linear thinking if we are to avoid ecological tragedy. This type of thinking emanates from the left side of the brain, the 'rational' side and is the kind that has been encouraged by western males. That is to say it has been seen as the highest form of mental functioning and has dominated our education system for centuries. It is a non-feeling way of functioning that removes us from the raw material that we are considering. It is the kind of thinking that we witness in the Eden myth and most Christian theology. This is not entirely surprising as it is a way of thinking that can be linked to the one-sided brain development of the male and after all they have dominated in matters of culture and religion.

There is ample evidence from psychology to show that males are more inclined to only develop the one side of the brain. They are unable to use both sides at once as women can. There are many theories as to why this may be but the most convincing is because of their late language development (Springer and Deutsch 1981: 121-30). This biological tendency has found its way into culture and has led to the predominance of dualistic thinking. Ruether highlights the problems that this has caused by focusing on agricultural methods. Linear thinking in agriculture leads to long rows of the same plant becoming more vulnerable to disease. Humans then compensate for the vulnerability they have caused through the use of chemicals which in turn poison the whole eco-system. The left brain method fails to see the wider implications. By acknowledging that there is no divine right involved in a dualistic view of the world, it is rather the ability to perceive only half the picture, we are able to move ahead with other ways of thinking and being.

Ruether is not suggesting that a return to nature in all her glorious harmony would be desirable or even possible. For her nature is fallen in the sense that we have intervened in its processes so much it has lost a certain amount of its innocence (1989: 149). The recreation of the earth and the people who inhabit it is a historical process that can be seen as redemptive. The Christian focus needs to change from salvation of the individual soul to that of redeeming the earth. This redemption is an unfolding story of people in mutual relation with the whole of the divine/created order. This calls for both the attention that McFague advocates and the conversion of intelligence that Ruether looks for. While neither writer is seeking to imply dualism their ideas may be taken that way. Intelligence has for so long been viewed as a function of the mind alone while attention lends itself to being viewed as residing in the mind. Therefore, perhaps an embodied way of relating with the world, one based on sensuous connection with the created order would avoid this tendency. This is not to imply dualism or to see women as merely physical but rather a call for new emphasis on feeling, interconnectedness and sensuality in the process of knowing. This does not in any way exclude rationality but does not give it priority, it becomes a function of the person that comes into play to help make sense of the feelings rather than override them.

Strange as it may seem there are pointers to this sensuous connection with the created order in the Genesis story. We are told that knowledge resides in the tree with the luscious fruit, the kind of fruit that one cannot resist touching and savouring. The young male god prohibits the eating of this fruit and dictates that all people need to know he will tell them. The goddess background to this story gives it a very different context and meaning. This young male god knows that he has to make this prohibition if he is to remain 'in charge' because once people have known in their bodies, touched, tasted, smelt knowledge, they cannot be easily controlled. The depth of knowledge that the whole body gives empowers people to stand firm in their convictions.

The Genesis story clearly shows that God provides food for people but they may 'use it' rather than be grateful to it and understand their obligations to the preservation of the resources, in the way encouraged by Celtic and native American religions. The older deity, the goddess, on the other hand encouraged people to get lost in the sensuous joys of creation and to celebrate all life forces. She was the one who enlivened the whole of creation and in engaging fully with creation humans were involved in honouring her. To eat of the fruit of the tree of knowledge would make the goddess rejoice, she would be satisfied that people were taking of her body and seeing that it was good. Further, in so doing they would be confirming the power of their own experience. Far from rooting them in over-personalized and isolating experiences this embodied knowing connects them with others and the divine.

It could be argued that Eve, our foremother, was not disobeying the divine but rather hearing an older divine voice. In exploring her garden home she was seeking knowledge of it on its own terms and not according to a 'given', a set of statements handed down from a disembodied Word. She is then a model for eco-theology, the one who encourages us to eat of the luscious fruit of the tree of knowledge and savour its goodness. Rather than remove ourselves from the world for the sake of our souls we should be embracing it as the tangible body of God that it is. This embrace should be one of mutuality not the strangle hold that patriarchy often confuses with affection. We should extend to the world the erotic connection that Heyward advocates between people. Christianity has not encouraged the inclusion of the world as subject in our process of divine becoming and it is time to redress that imbalance.

Of course an understanding of connections between people and the land is not alien to African, Asian and native American traditions. Here we witness peoples who ask permission from the ground before unrooting any living thing. They understand that people do not have a right to take anything. and so when they do they must not take more than is really needed. Further, they should replace what they can in order to show both gratitude and respect to nature. If we dare to incorporate this way of being into western thought we have a radically different picture. One that can begin to imagine erotic connection between people and the earth because the earth is no longer dead but infused with life and meaning. We can then,

> begin to feel deep respect, even a sense of awe before the life-giving, yet fragile interwovenness of the earth... The rhythmic ebb and flow of the rivers and sea becomes God's dance. The life-giving fecundity of the land with the water is the source of food coming from God's bosom... God energizes the cosmos, and the cosmos in return moves with the creator in a cosmic dance of exquisite balance and beauty (Chung Hyun Kyung in Hallman 1994: 177).

To include the world in our erotic and embodied process will mean that we give up the desire for authority and control over it as we realize that we are simply part of the process and not the pinnacle of creation. It will enable us to realize that we are part of a bigger whole and the vulnerability we feel with this realization is just the way it is, we should not seek ways to lessen the tension but simply to live with it. What an erotic connection with the earth does is make us realize that a 'greener' life style also has implications for others on the planet, it helps them to survive. Paradoxically, if we lessen our fanatical attempts to control and survive we make the survival of all a more viable option.

Ecotheology should move away from the idea that we are faced with a series of problems that need solving. Admittedly, this problem solving is often less violent to nature when advocated by ecotheologians but nonetheless it seems the wrong way to think of things. It should be replaced by an erotic connection with nature that thrives on respect, acceptance, mutuality, humility and joy. A connection that empowers us to act for the earth even to the point of sacrifice. When we disconnect our heads from our bodies we are able to sustain an ecological approach that demands more and more from the earth and believes that all the 'problems' will be solvable. However, when we connect erotically with mind and body together we are compelled to nurture and heal rather than dominate and destroy.

When we realize that nothing is guaranteed we are, paradoxically, in a stronger position than when living in a theological 'disney world' where the good guys get their reward in the end. To abandon dualistic thinking places the emphasis more squarely on the here and now and frees us to seek empowerment-in-relation with all that is around us. Instead of looking for the divine beyond what we see, we have to pay more attention to what we see in order to engage bodily with the divine in its diversity around and within us. Christians have to come to terms with the stark reality that redemption does not lie beyond this world and this body but within both. Ecotheology is a theology of redemption not just an ethical issue tagged on at the end of Christian systematic theology. It will be a long time before the malestream in theology understands that incarnational theology makes escape from the created order unlikely. By placing the tree from Eden rather than that from Calvary at the centre of a theology of redemption it is hoped that people will embrace the reality of the here and now. Further it will show that the garden has yet to be understood and nurtured rather than a harvest already planted has just to be cut and gathered. There is a process unfolding and the tree that was once the symbol of fallenness is best reimaged as that of our ecological future if that unfolding is to preserve the planet and its inhabitants.

Chapter Seven

Directions in Body Theology

In arguing for a radical understanding of incarnation that places the divine solidly in the world and challenges any notions of dualism we are raising many questions. Some of the areas affected by this approach are life after death, economics and sacramental theology. We have in other chapters suggested the way in which 'radical incarnation' will affect sexual and ecological understandings. In this final chapter we explore some of the implications and outworkings of body theology for and in Christian theology, as well as attempting some kind of provisional assessment of the body theology as it has developed so far.

Life after Death: The Final Phallacy?

Belief in life after death was widespread in the ancient world and the Hebrew Scriptures provide us with a variety of responses to the problem. The semitic world view was rather different to our own seeing the cosmos as divided into three layers—earth, heaven and the netherworld. This enabled a belief that those in either the higher (gods) or lower (the dead) regions could intervene in human affairs. To die simply meant to change one's place in the cosmic structure so that while there was physical decay something of the person remained, personality traits and memory for example (1 Sam. 28.10-14). The quality of life that one had after death depended on the life led on earth and the vigilance of one's children in carrying out rituals. The dead either resided in the lighter, upper parts of Sheol or the lower more squalid parts (Isa. 14.4-21). Those who resided in the upper parts were given the title 'gods' (1 Sam. 28.13; Ps. 16.3) as they could intervene in people's lives in startling ways. Private rituals were carried out to keep the dead happy and to ensure they remained in the upper regions of Sheol where they could be most effective for the living.

The later biblical writers condemned ancestor worship and speaking to the dead at the same time as advocating the worship of the one true God. This was possibly as much to do with attempting to create a national identity under pressure from outside forces as it was to do with theological insight. The outcome of these condemnations was that the living and the dead became totally separated and the bodies of the dead were viewed as unclean. The dead were seen as existing in a dark and gloomy place but at least they were free from the trials of the earth (Job 3.17-19). However, there is also the notion that once removed from life people are also removed from the worship of Yahweh (Sir. 17.22-23), they were godless and alone. In fact as the religion of Yahweh developed death came to be seen as the end of being. However, this belief saw a turn-around and once again political expectation and theology interacted to produce a belief in the resurrection of the body. While the nation itself was gradually being wiped off the map the people nevertheless clung to the promises of God that they would be a great nation. Their hope for liberation coupled with their encounter with Zoroastrian religion led to a new hope. Between 585 and 568 BCE Ezekiel delivered a series of hope filled visions in which he saw a new Jerusalem and the dry bones of the dead raised to life. The plain of dry bones that Ezekiel claims to have seen may indeed have been a Zoroastrian burial ground since they left bodies to be devoured by birds and the bones to be bleached by the sun. They believed that the creator would reassemble the bones at the final resurrection. Ezekiel no doubt knew of this belief and used it for his own purposes. Whereas Zoroastrians expected a renewed universe Ezekiel looked for a new Jerusalem with the people free from foreign oppression (McDannell and Lang 1988: 12-13). It is not entirely clear whether Ezekiel thought this resurrection would last for ever but others who came later believed that it had a limited time span, for example Enoch thought it lasted five hundred years and then people died again (1 En. 10.10). Despite its non-eternal quality this kind of resurrection still helped people make sense out of their present suffering and their apparently unconcerned God.

There were those, however, who appeared to deny death altogether such as Elijah and Enoch who were assumed into heaven. It was their example that is taken up in Psalm 73 with the author musing that what is possible for those holy men is possible for all. Thus residing with God in heaven rather than languishing in Sheol became a real hope for all. The idea had entered the religious arena that one's relationship with

God, if it was strong enough, could not be broken by death. This high-lights the importance of the individual in the development of Jewish thought, marking a move from corporate identity and development of the notion of individual punishment or reward. While Jewish thought emphasized the relationship between God and the people as a whole there was no need for the idea of life after death with reward or pun-ishment for the individual but once the relationship became more per-sonal, because justice was not seen to be done to the deserving race, what happened to the individual after death became a more pressing matter. Jewish thought was not immune to Greek influence and we witness an increasing concern with the nature of the soul, the Book of Wisdom taking it for granted that the soul exists and is strong while Philo of Alexandria developed his thinking to the point of saying that life is just a brief and unfortunate interlude that interrupts the true higher existence of the soul. 'Soul preparation' took the place of polit-ical action and ideas about the resurrection of the state. By the time Christianity emerged there was a rich variety of thought available on the subject of the after life.

It is therefore not extraordinary that early Christianity would have views on this matter. Romans 1.3-4 states that it was the resurrection that turned Jesus of Nazareth into the Christ. Further, it is the belief of many contemporary Christians that if there was no resurrection from the dead then there can be no Christianity. We see therefore that the issue of what happens after death is a crucial one for Christianity. One of the most telling gospel passages concerning this matter is where Jesus is presented with the case of a woman who marries several brothers as each leaves her childless and so in fulfilment of Jewish law each brother takes her as his wife. Jesus is asked whose wife she will be in heaven. The Saducees who asked the question would think that it highlighted the absurdity of the beliefs about life after death held by some of their contemporaries. Although Jesus' answer assumes there is life after death his insistence that there will be no marriage and offspring challenges the apocalyptic perspective of many at the time. His answer suggests that those who are dead do not have to wait in order to inherit a renewed earth but can enjoy heaven immediately. Further, body was not essential for eternal life. However, in contrast we are also faced with the resur-rection stories which are at pains to point out that Jesus has risen with his body. Although he is reported to have the ability to appear through walls and doors (Jn 20.26) and is often not instantly recognizable

(Jn 21.1-14) he can be touched and does still bear the scars received at death as well as appearing to still have a healthy appetite. After his appearances Jesus ascended into heaven and it is unclear whether he kept his body.

A significant contribution was made to the debate by Paul. He believed that at death the person sleeps and at a later time is reunited with God. The dead would be bodily resurrected and enjoy life in a kingdom where God rules eternally. In this way he appears to differ from the Jesus of the gospel accounts who thinks that heaven can be entered at death. The resurrected bodies are, however, spiritual. Those who are alive at the time of the final judgment will be transformed into spiritual beings in the twinkling of an eye. Paul is unclear as to how these bodies would look but he is very clear that heaven involves dwelling in the presence of God forever.

The Fathers generally felt that bodily resurrection was necessary for a number of reasons. Aquinas argued that we are not really people if we do not have bodies while Tertullian maintained that justice demands that we are judged as a whole. Further, he claimed that nature itself demands resurrection since it is made for humans and is continually renewed. Therefore it would be a nonsense to suggest that humans could perish as nature keeps blooming for us (Badham 1976: 53-54). The Fathers presumed that the resurrection of the flesh was taught throughout the Bible and as we have seen this is not correct. Despite their insistence on the resurrection of the body they also agreed that this was nothing compared to the bliss that believers would eventually have in heaven. Augustine in the City of God views resurrection as restoration of bodily wholeness with the added bonus of incorruptibility. He thought we would rise aged thirty with gender and possibly the most virtuous would be transparent to show off their harmoniously arranged livers and intestines (Bynum 1995: 100).

Much of the Christian material shows a fear of being swallowed by the natural processes of decay. Death was seen as disgusting as it meant that people had surrendered uncontrollably to the functions of the body. Further, there was a fear that people could not keep their personality if there was not a body to attach it to. Hildegard however conveys the idea that there can be organic change without threat to the self (Bynum 1995: 159). The thirteenth century saw the introduction of the practice of dissecting saints and burying their parts in different places. Yet at the same time two Councils, the fourth Lateran and Lyon, were affirming that all rise with the bodies that they now wear. This would leave God with a huge reassembling task and logic would dictate that keeping body parts together was the best solution.

Christian feminist liberation theologians have a varied and rich tradition to consider. Not a great deal has been written about life after death, possibly because the problems of this world have seemed paramount. However, those such as Heyward have been careful to avoid dualistic thinking when dealing with resurrection. She sees resurrection as what happens to those who align themselves with the praxis of Jesus and stubbornly refuse to give up intimacy and immediacy with God. This is why she feels Christianity may call itself a resurrection faith. Ruether believes it to be of fundamental importance that we give up notions of eternal survival (1995) since this androcentric obsession has almost caused the destruction of the world. Many Christian feminists are highly suspicious of eschatology, arguing that in its most individualistic form it reflects a particularly male concern with the independent, isolated self and has contributed towards the ecological crisis:

> By pretending that we can immortalize ourselves, our souls, and perhaps even our bodies for some future resurrection, we are immortalizing our garbage and polluting the earth. If we are really to learn to recycle our garbage as fertilizer for new growth, our waste as matter for new artefacts, we need a spirituality of recycling that accepts ourselves as part of that process of growth, decay, reintegration into the earth and new growth (Ruether 1995: 61).

For Ruether human consciousness is part of this process of disintegration, returning to 'a great consciousness underlying the whole of life process that carries and expands with the remembering of each of our small selves, while letting go of the illusion of immortal self within each of our many moral embodiments' (Ruether 1995: 61). There is no sense here of human beings falling into nothingness. Rather human beings move from one form of existence into another, one form of embodiment to another in the body of God. Salvation ceases to be a matter for the next world and becomes instead a matter of flourishing in this world.

It seems to many feminist theologians that once we abandon the illusions of dualism and unchanging absolutes we are in a healthier position. That is, we no longer have to fear change as being outside the realm of the divine, in fact it is the nature of the divine. Death then is merely reintegration of our body into the earth, a very physical merging with the energy that we have called divine but without any sense of personal identity or 'me-ness' continuing. Change is holy and we should embrace it rather than trying to halt what is natural by appealing to intellectual tricks. This is not to say that we wish to abandon the symbol of resurrection but rather see it as a more urgent and embodied reality in the here and now. By harnessing the erotic power of which we have already spoken it seems that resurrection can become the symbol for the transformation of the cosmos and the ruptured experiences of people. The business of creating a new heaven and earth is the business of now and resurrection should follow the numerous crucifixions we see around us daily. The women at the cross remained vigilant throughout the pain and the hopelessness and wept, mourned, grieved and hurt in a new dawn, this may be the meaning of resurrection in feminist theology. Perhaps feminist theology is going back to ancient biblical concepts or just reading the signs of the times but personal salvation is not of the utmost importance in the world as we see it today, cosmic resurrection is, and it is a task we all have to undertake as co-redeemers of creation. Our 'reward' in this is to have lived in such a way that 'the children's teeth are not set on edge'.

Whether such an understanding of life after death adequately accounts for an embodied longing for immortality in God, whether it is an adequate reinterpretation of the tradition's emphasis on the continuity and discontinuity for the resurrected body, whether it offers a sufficiently embodied account of life after death and whether it fails to take account of the life experience of those who, because of social, economic and ecological situation die young and have no chance to flourish (unlike most western middle-class people), is an issue that body theology will have to address.

Capitalism: The Ethic of Death

Women are sick of mopping up the wounds of advanced capitalism and wish a halt to be called. These wounds gashed into the lives of people by the many headed beast of multinational corporations are diverse ranging from inhuman working conditions and wages to unreasonable demands on human time and the world's resources. The influence of these institutions is enormous. They affect education by dictating what kind of knowledge is useful, they influence foreign policy and create the very fabric of our lives. They preach loyalty and conformity yet show little loyalty to anything but profit. If a company withdraws from an area that it may well have created by its arrival the impact is devastating, but if the profit margins are better elsewhere there is no bargaining to be done. These beasts of advanced capitalism wish to have control but no responsibility. A dramatic example of this is the Kerr-McGee corporation which was negligent in its handling of plutonium and falsified records to hide its incompetence. The company had 3300 violations against its name and was only penalized eight times. In this case one employee who had drawn attention to the abuses was killed before she was able to give final evidence, still nothing was done.

Countries can be ruined by a multinational changing its marketing strategy. Cash cropping is a well-known example of how countries that are surviving by the skin of their teeth are pushed right to the brink. Third World countries have inherited a very fragile and finely balanced economic/ecological/survival base. This is the legacy of colonialism that ripped the guts out of balanced ways of life. These countries have now been made dependent on the capitalist world in large part for their survival. Sadly there is no sense of responsibility on the part of the multinationals that exploit the developing world. What they leave behind is not only unemployment but usually a devastated region. Areas are routinely left with no income and no way of returning to the subsistence farming that sustained the people for generations. The mythology that the West develops for coping with this gross exploitation is that developing countries always have high mortality rates due to famine, disease and floods. Natural disasters have to date been more prevalent in developing countries but strategies had been created to deal with these. Under first the weight of colonialism and now multinational intervention they have lost these coping traditions and are left more vulnerable than ever. Advanced capitalism needs consumers and the developing world is a target. The appeal in the advertising is to the superior nature of white values and the old-fashioned ways of the indigenous population. This can have devastating consequences as in the case of powdered milk for babies. These children are already malnourished and need their mothers' milk, the mothers however falsely often believe that the more sophisticated western powdered variety is better. The West comes to the rescue by providing medicines; the snag is that they are either of an inferior quality or cost on average 155 per cent more than in USA or Britain. Along with the medicines we also export as much of our pollution as possible. That is we set up the most polluting factories in Third

World countries or actually put waste on ships and export it. The consequences for local people are devastating—ill health and high death rates are the real cost of this export trade.

There is no doubt that bodies are speaking out under this system. Those under the most crushing exploitation are simply dying while even those of the so-called privileged group are beginning to suffer. Advanced capitalism is a system that exists based on the illusion of security, it is not ultimately self-sustaining nor has it an interest in sustaining people who are not useful to it. The net result is that stress related cancer is on the increase, heart disease is flourishing as are all kinds of mystery viruses. The more successful a person is in the corporate world the more likely it is that they will die soon after retirement. The economic system that we perpetuate is killing us all, when will we listen to our bodies? Unfortunately the churches do not tend to speak out about this system. Indeed much American right wing religion favours advanced capitalism and advises its adherents that riches are a sign of God's grace. The reality is, however, that capitalism breeds genocidal myopia. Western governments back wars in order to advance their own agendas as was clearly seen in the case of the USA and Nicaragua. Despite being found guilty of unlawful involvement in the Contra wars and ordered to pay $17 billion incompensation, the USA refuses and continues to make economic life almost impossible for the Nicaraguans.

Ethicists have to find ways of hearing the body and upturning these systems of exploitation. Perhaps a starting point is Marx's notion of sensuous labour, that is a system where the worker is connected with that which is produced in such a way as to bring about satisfaction and a just reward. Advanced capitalism separates the means of production from the product so that people are no longer connected with what they create. This leads to soul destroying work but large 'cost effective' plants. The bodies of people are highlighting the fact that the troubles that people have are not just limited to them, that is, it is not just the individual that does not fit the system, rather we have a system that does not fit the people. We find ourselves agreeing with Harrison when she says:

> Since for us the arena of divine/human relations is the very mundane, flesh and blood world,we have no problem with the assumption that sensuous labour and bread are even more foundational to the life of the spirit than is prayer (1985: 75).

To achieve both these goals it will not be sufficient to simply redistribute wealth, we need a new form of production born out of radical vision. The starting point for that vision is human experience, not capital.

'Hope's Last Weapon': Laughter

Most theological reflection upon the body has focused on two areas—sexuality and gender, and ecology. Recently, however, reflection on the embodied experience of laughter has begun to emerge. Reflection upon the experience of laughter may help us discern more clearly both the potential and limitations of body theology.

As far as we can tell only human beings laugh. Laughter is induced either by some kind of interaction between the body and the mind or by some agitation of the body itself. In either case it is a bodily reaction. Why human beings laugh is a question that has exercised minds of scientists, philosophers and sociologists for centuries. Gilhus collapses these reflections into three major theories: (1) the superiority theory which links laughter to power over another; (2) the incongruity theory which attributes the laughter to the bringing together of two opposite meanings; in such a way as to produce an unexpected meaning; (3) the relief theory which claims that laughter is a means of relief from the psychological pressure of keeping certain things taboo, a form of safety valve which in allowing pressure to be occasionally released keeps the taboos and order of a society in place (Gilhus 1997: 5). Gilhus notes that all of these theories assume that laughter is a universal, disembodied phenomenon, but it is not: laughter takes on a different meaning in different cultures, just as the body does.

Indeed, the understanding of laughter in a particular culture is intimately related to that culture's understanding of the symbolic meaning of the body. Understandings of laughter in the ancient cultures that cradled Christianity were characterized by ambiguity. Ancient Near Eastern societies associated laughter with the erotic and with the process of creating and recreating the world. The eruptive nature of laughter coupled with the wide opening of the mouth that usually accompanies laughter led ancient Greek cultures to connect laughter with the sexual and the cults of Demeter, Aphrodite and Dionysos involved much laughter and obscenity. Laughter was then one of the ways in which the human body reflected and partook in the cosmological process of creation and recreation. But laughter was also a means of social control. The gods certainly laughed but they laughed at, rather than with,

human beings—at their weakness and stupidity. Both Plato and Aristotle
sought to decentralize laughter. For Plato laughter was unethical because
it largely arises from an aggressive pleasure in the unconscious inferiority
of another. Laughter was also a threat to the moderation and dignity that
was necessary for an ethical life.[1] Plato's disciple, Aristotle, followed him
in this concern that laughter could destabilize but even though
Aristotle's extensive study of comedy has been lost it is possible to pick
up from his other works a less negative attitude to laughter than Plato.
Recognizing that laughter is a distinctive characteristic of humanity,
Aristotle realized its usefulness as a tool in debate and as a means of
relaxing. The issue for Aristotle was what kind of laughter was appropriate for a free man—certainly not the uncontrolled, vulgar hilarity of
the buffoon. He came to the conclusion that irony was superior to buffoonery and humourlessness because it was an understated, modest and
moderate form of humour.[2] Aristotle's recognition that laughter is a
useful rhetorical device was echoed in Roman philosophers who used
laughter to question the religious beliefs and practices that characterized
the culture of the Roman empire in late antiquity.

The associations of laughter with fertility cults, doubt, the unethical
and illiberal in the ancient Near East did nothing to endear it to the
early Christian theologians. They also inherited a biblical tradition
which in many respects was suspicious of laughter. The wisdom tradition in particular associated laughter with the rejection of wisdom Sir.
21.14-15 and 27.12-13). Many of the early theologians concluded that
immoderate laughter left the body out of control and open to sin. Early
monastic rules are full of warnings of the dangers of laughter and pun-
ishments for those who succumb to it (Gilhus 1997: 60-68). Weeping,
on the other hand, was approved of because it was considered to be an
appropriate reaction to sin and the redemptive suffering and death of
Jesus. John Chrysostom famously claimed that Jesus never laughed but
he did weep and also declared that those who mourn are blessed.[3] Some
laughter was considered a sign of holiness, the laughter of ascetics at the
tricks demons tried unsuccessfully to play upon them and the laughter of
spiritual joy which demonstrated the extent to which the person's body
had already been transfigured into a near resurrection state of joy
(Gilhus 1997: 69). One factor which certainly led to a distrust of

---

1. Plato, *Republic* 2-3.
2. Aristotle, *Nicomachaen Ethics* 4.4 and *Rhetoric* 18.7.
3. John Chrysostom, *Homilies on the Gospel of Matthew* 6.5-6.

laughter among many early Christian theologians was the Gnostic use of laughter. In their writings the Gnostics ridiculed and mocked their opponents and so laughter became in their philosophy a symbol of *gnosis*. This is particularly clear in their theology of the laughing saviour— the eternal Christ who did not suffer or die on the cross but substituted Simon of Cyrene and looked on laughing at the ignorance of humanity running after the material Jesus rather than the pure spiritual saviour.[4] The Gnostics therefore associated laughter with knowledge of radical body/soul dualism.

Yet, despite many theologians' suspicions of laughter the Church could never keep it down. The focus on joy in the New Testament (particularly the Gospel of Luke) and the promise of laughter in the coming reign of God (Lk. 6.22) prevented a complete marginalization of laughter. The mediaeval period with its increased emphasis upon embodiment in the sacraments and the lives and relics of the saints also saw controlled expressions of laughter in a sacred context. The earthy comedy of the English Mystery Plays written to be performed during the feast of Corpus Christ is well known. Much of the humour in those plays is focused on the body and the failure of various people to grasp the nature of the incarnation. The Feast of Fools widely celebrated throughout the West on 1 January throughout the mediaeval period in Europe, but particularly associated with France, was a feast of outrageous buffoonery in which the lower clergy ridiculed the higher clergy, dressed as animals and women, ran around the churches, brayed like donkeys, and mocked the liturgy (Chambers 1954). There are several ways of interpreting the feast. It could be understood simply as a controlled explosion of the tension that accumulated in a highly structured Church with an ambiguous attitude to the body and women. By barely tolerating this annual eruption the hierarchy actually managed to keep order the rest of the year. But the feast's positioning in the wake of the feast of the incarnation suggests that there may have been other forces behind the laughter. The story of the nativity reminds all who celebrate it of the raising of the lowly and the casting down of the mighty, of the messy reality of God become human in female flesh to inaugurate a reign which overturns all human values. The Feast of Fools could be interpreted as an explosion of incarnational energy, the laughter as an integral part of that explosion exposed the extent to which the Church

4.   *The Second Treaty of the Great Seth*, CG, 7.2. 55.30-56: 19.

failed to realize in its own organization and beliefs the reality of the incarnation (Gilhus 1997: 78-88).

An outpouring of resurrection spirit in the form of laughter took place in the German-speaking mediaeval world at Easter. The *risus paschalis* (Easter Laughter) consisted of preachers reducing their congregations to fits of laughter through bawdy humour (Kuschel 1994: 83-87). This laughter must have expressed many things: relief at the vindication of Christ, joy at the defeat of death and delight in the transfiguration of the body. A modern poet has described the resurrection as 'a laugh freed for ever and for ever'.[5]

With the Reformation and Enlightenment came a renewed distrust of laughter as an enemy of reason but the post-modern world has found a place for laughter. Psychologists tell us that laughter is good for us and philosophers too have redeemed laughter. Perhaps the most famous modern treatise on laughter is in the form of a historical detective novel, Umberto Eco's *The Name of the Rose* (1980). An English friar, William of Baskerville, investigates a series of murders in an Italian Benedictine monastery in which are hidden Aristotle's lost reflections upon laughter as an instrument for uncovering truth. Jorge, the blind librarian who does all he can to keep the manuscript hidden aligns himself with John Chrysostom—to him laughter is an expression and force of doubt, the enemy of truth. Laughter threatens the religious, moral and social order because it is base, associated with the belly rather than the brain, the plebeian rather than the masters. But the very experience of trying to solve the murders has convinced William that human beings are misguided in their attempts to establish a clearly defined and stable divine order in the world. And so he remarks to his pupil Adso, 'Perhaps the mission of those who love mankind is to make people laugh at the truth, to make truth laugh, because the only truth lies in learning to free ourselves from the insane passion for truth' (Eco 1980: 491). For William laughter is the embodied recognition of the ultimate omnipotence and freedom of the divine that makes a mockery of all human attempts to order the world in God's name. For many post-modern theologians this is the body's grace, its resistance to totalitarian truths, its 'wild wisdom' resisting the 'will-to-truth' which seeks to establish immutable truths,

---

5.   Patrick Kavanagh, 'Lough Derg' cited in Hardy and Ford 1984: 73.

only through the suppression or oppression of the sensual, that is those markings of culture subject to the limitations and vicissitudes of finite existence which engage the senses of sight, sound, touch, smell and taste. Thus, the site for new thinking or reconstruction is just those 'sensual remainders' or 'sensate markings of culture' that survive the clash between forces of the 'will-to-truth' and their opposition (MacDonald 1995: 118-19).

MacDonald goes on to note that any attempt to do theology out of these sensual remainders will lead not to a new metaphysics but to an 'aesthetics of existence' which resists the dualism of the subject and object but which is born out of an 'eros of the limits, (which) does not seek to absorb or exterminate the "other" as the eros of binary thinking must do' (MacDonald 1995: 129) but constantly destabilizes the subject, opening it to the other. This approach resists both the 'nay-sayers' like Jorge who are against the body and identify the humanly constructed order with the divine and the 'yea-sayers' who claim that the body is a site of repressed natural goodness, the shadow of the dominant order which is associated with truth, (the gay to the straight, the female to the male, the earth to culture) and simply reverse the power-dynamics already in play, becoming as dangerous as the nay-sayers. This form of theological reflection is rather rooted in the margins of culture, in the

> 'sensate markings' or practices of culture operating in the 'in-between' of everyday life. It is the graffiti of subway stations, the design of public spaces and buildings, the rhymes of children playing hopscotch, the jokes shared at the coffee pot. It is black leather jackets and pierced eyebrows— a whole realm of markings which we tend to pass by in our workday lives as we focus on other things. But at the edge of our vision, they persist. And through the lure of the dance of colour, scent, texture and form, these markings at the edge of our awareness reveal the dynamic of cultural meanings in various stages of formation and deformation. It is the 'sensate markings' of our lives which seduce us out of the ruts of habituated thinking and being (MacDonald 1995: 136).

The theologian examines these not to establish some universal truth from reflection upon them nor to apply some universal truth to them in the process of interpretation but in order to understand what forces are at work in them and to draw attention to the possibilities for a loving and transforming encounter with 'the other' within them. In this type of body theology the divine is not a stable being either inside or outside the world but a 'wild being', untamed, an 'eternal recurrence of difference' that opens possibilities for wild love.

This post-modern understanding of laughter recognizes and attempts to avoid the pitfalls of some other forms of body theology which identify the divine with an unconstructed, innocent natural body which has to be discovered and uncovered. The problem with such an approach is that it can lead to a complete identification between the divine and human bodily experience as interpreted by one group or another. In other words there is an annihilation of difference and with difference the very bodily desire which most body theologians want to claim is the royal road to the divine. Desire, most post-modern philosophers agree, is born of difference. The need to emphasize this difference is obvious when we consider laughter in terms of body theology. Not all laughter is subversive, it can be a weapon of conformity. Laughter can be used to ridicule the victims of social systems, it can be used to stir up hate, it can be an expression of scorn. Karl-Josef Kuschel reminds us of the use that Hitler and the Nazi regime made of comedy:

> With jokes about Jews, anti-Semitic ploys, caricatures and not least with the help of entertainment films, the Fascists knew how to use laughter as a drug. A programmed Germany literally laughed itself to death while soldiers were being butchered by the hundred thousand at the front, hundreds of cities were being exterminated in the nights, and millions of Jews were being gassed in the concentration camps. Indeed Jewish jokes had prepared for the pogroms; here too laughter had lowered the threshold of shame and removed the inhibitions which should have been there. That made the work of the executioners all the easier (Kuschel 1994: 123-24).

The early Church fathers were right to recognize that laughter can be both a sign of divine grace and a sign of alienation from the divine. Sometimes the refusal to laugh, to assume a closed bodily position is an incarnation of divine grace.

However, there is grace in laughter, which can be illustrated by the story of Abraham and Sarah (Gen. 17). Both are people of faith yet when they are told they are to have a child their bodily reaction is to laugh, even as Abraham falls on his face in a position of worship, he laughs. His body expresses both doubt and faith in one movement. Neither are punished for this doubt but are rewarded with a son, Isaac (which means 'God laughs'), and out of this curious interaction between human embodiment and divine embodiment the people of Israel are born—born out of laughter. Karl-Josef Kuschel argues that Christian laughter, a laughter that 'body's forth' from being incorporated into the body of Christ is, in Harvey Cox's words 'hope's last weapon' (Cox 1969) because

> Christians who laugh are expressing their feeling that the facts of the world are not the end of the matter, though this world need not be despised. Christians who laugh are taking part in God's laughter at his creation and his creatures, and this laughter is a laughter of mercy and friendliness. Christians who laugh are expressing resistance to a 'postmodern' ideology in which everything is optional, to an aesthetic of indifference, and to a fanatical mania about the truth and the use of violent terrorism to defend the truth. Christians who laugh are insisting that the stories of the world's sufferings do not have the last word, and are also offering sufficient opportunity to penetrate an attitude of 'postmodern optionalism' and an aesthetics of irony and enunciation to show solidarity with those who having nothing to laugh about in this world (Kuschel 1994: 133).

The Body as Sacrament

Christianity of the mediaeval period provides us with a rich tradition of embodiment. This was the time when the cult of relics proliferated. However, it was not only the bodies of dead saints that were felt to hold miraculous powers but the bodies of the living. Holy people spat or blew into the mouths of others to cure or to convey grace. While some even washed in the bath water of the holy. Many of the Holy Virgins from the Low Country lactated miraculously and the faithful were cured by taking this milk to drink. Further, the cult of the holy foreskin was popular at this time with a Beguine, Agnes Blannbekin, recording that she took it in her mouth and it tasted as sweet as honey (Bynum 1991: 186). Catherine of Siena however marries Christ with his foreskin used as the wedding ring. It is not at all unusual at this time for women to taste God, to deeply kiss Christ or enter his heart and bathe in his blood. These were very physical times! Hadewijch spoke of being so deeply penetrated by Christ that she lost herself in ecstatic love. While the male mystics were 'at one' with Christ the women were so deeply affected that they moved beyond their senses. Theirs was a very direct way of 'stating that experiencing Christ turns on the bodily senses of the receiving mystic' (Bynum 1991: 192).

Despite having the ability to experience Christ so intimately the female body was still treated with suspicion. It was after all still the site of the sin of Eve and was not perfect enough to represent Christ at the altar. On the other hand many female mystics were viewed as being the flesh of Christ as their bodies could do what his had done, that is, bleed, feed, die and give life to others (Bynum 1991: 222). The picture we get therefore is not a clear one and this is in part due to the fact that we are receiving both a clerical and a lay account of how things were perceived. While Aquinas could advocate the venerating of a body for the soul that it once housed, the ordinary folk were very happy with venerating the body.

The holy body then was in some sense sacramental in that it conveyed grace to believers. It is always very tricky to use the word sacrament and be sure of the meaning conveyed. Of course, there is no mention of the word in the Christian Scriptures although there are many actions considered to be symbolic and significant for the Christian community. The generally accepted definition of sacrament these days is 'an outward and visible sign of an inward and spiritual (invisible) grace' (Goudy 1996: 209). In this sense then there seems no reason to suggest that the body cannot act in this sacramental way. The difficulty that some feminist theologians may have with the standard definition of a sacrament is that it appears to place more meaning on what is not seen than on what is. It lends itself to dualism, although it does not have to. Sacraments stand as a testimony to the bringing together of God and the created order. Feminist theologians would not wish to challenge this but may simply wish to lay different emphasis in the interpretation of this weaving and dancing of divine matter.

Leonardo Boff argues that one of the reasons that Christianity cannot agree with Marxism is that it sees matter as sacramental not as merely for manipulation and exploitation (1987: 4). He argues that sacraments arise from human interaction and only really take shape in the process of encounter. They then enable the person to transcend the situation and become present to a higher reality which is God (1987: 5-6). In a sense they are 'performance orientated' as they aim at altering the way in which people behave. They illustrate a past and a hoped-for future in the reality of the present. They are meant to draw us into the world but also point us beyond it. For example, the bread of the eucharist is meant to bring to mind something that is not bread. As Boff puts it, 'the bread becomes transparent, revealing a transcendent reality' (1987: 24). In this way it brings together transcedence and immanence and Boff claims it is no longer like any other bread since it ceases to be only immanent. This applies not just to eucharistic bread, everything that points us to transcendence ceases to be itself. Anything that becomes a sacrament embodies a whole experience in which transcendence and immanenceare no longer distinct categories. Rather, by the transcendent breaking through into the immanent the latter becomes transparent and the reality of God is seen clearly. When the transparency is lost so is the sacramental value (1987: 25).

Boff's work is encouraging as he is well aware that sacraments should not move people away from the world but enable them to look more closely at it. For him struggles for liberation are sacramental and so in a real sense history itself can be seen in this way. However, the difficulties with this position are shown by Boff, unintentionally, when he speaks of Christ being active in the world even if there were no church:

> But if there were no church, no community of believers, there would be
> no one to draw him out of anonymity, to decipher his present but hid-
> den reality, to pronounce his true name, and to venerate him as Liberator
> of human beings and Lord of the cosmos (1987: 52).

His understanding is exposed as exclusivist as well as demeaning of immanence. Matter, it appears, has meaning as long as it is able to reveal its real core, and that is Christ. This is the same dualistic problem that is encountered in the work of Nelson and is in many ways an inevitable outcome of Christian theology. Incarnation is never quite taken seriously enough, that is, matter still has to be infused or transformed if God is to be revealed in it. This seems to fly in the face of genuine incarnational understanding.

Incarnational theology should find no difficulty in declaring the body as sacrament. Indeed, much of what Boff and others say about sacraments lends itself to a body appreciation. What more than the human body and its needs makes us present in the world? What reminds us constantly of the demands of relationship more than our body selves? In what other ways can we really become aware of the divine than by looking deeply and bravely into the face of divine matter? This looking does not make something descend that is not otherwise present; it rather makes demands and offers empowerment in the light of divine indwelling. Bodies are the divine presence on earth, they are sacramental and are often profaned. All the created order pulsates with divine reality and needs no transformation to make it so. Profanity is not the failure to open oneself to outside intervention but rather the failure to love passionately all that we see, touch, taste, smell and hear. The sacramental process can then be understood as the spiralling liberation that such passion brings as well as resistance, based on body passion, in the face of profanity. Those committed to an incarnational religion should surely be committed to (and worship) the power, the passion, the pain, the sorrow, the joy and the mystery and majesty of the human body and the body of creation. This is not a religious 'body beautiful', cult of the individual, since it involves a passionate embrace of others, including the unlovely. A sacrament then is a celebration or mourning of things as they are, it is part of the process of divine becoming. A moment when we take stock, smile or weep, and move on. Sacraments, in a sense, reveal us to ourselves as well as to others, they are in this way moments of the disclosure of divine matter. Seven could never be enough, the cosmos sings with sacramental life!

Human Nature and the Future

One of the aims of body theology is to help the Church to construct a new anthropology, a new understanding of human nature, that recognizes the centrality of embodiment. Dermot Lane has outlined the steps that the Church will have to take in constructing such an anthropology (Lane 1995). First, the Church will have to accept the relational self, 'indeed, it must be said that relationality is a primary category, a fundamental characteristic of all beings in the world and not just human beings' (Lane 1995: 19). It is out of this relationality that individuality emerges and that individuality can only be maintained through continuous relationality. The self, like the body, is in a constant process of change as a result of its interaction with 'otherness' but there is also an underlying recognizable continuity.

Secondly, the Church must recognize that 'human beings belong to each other in an extraordinary degree of natural solidarity and social togetherness. This strong sense of solidarity can be seen not only at the human level but also on a wider cosmic scale in the light of the emerging common creation story' (Lane 1995: 22). This leads to a third step, the cosmic nature of human embodiment. Post-modern science has taught us that humans are made from the ashes of dead stars and that, 'the eye that searches the Milky Way galaxy is itself an eye shaped by the Milky Way. The mind that searches for contact with Milky Way is the very mind of the Milky Way in search of inner depths' (Swimme and Berry 1992: 45). This profound cosmic unity is not only rooted in the past but in the present: all bodies, cosmic, animal and human have an effect upon one another and that effect can reach across space and time (Sheldrake 1981: 13). This discovery opens up the possibilities for reformulating ancient Christian doctrines, such as the real presence of Christ in the eucharist and the communion of saints, in ways that reflect this cosmology and not a dualistic anthropology and theology. As Prokes has noted, 'If electrons from our bodies are, in statistical probability, now at the far reaches of the Milky Way, what must this mean concerning the sacramental presence of the Risen Christ in the Eucharist?' (Prokes 1996: 144). The fourth step in the development of a new anthropology that Lane identifies is a recognition of the social and communal nature of human beings (Lane 1995: 24). Lane goes on to assert that such an alternative anthropology is fundamentally eschatological. If we are going to emphasize the relational nature of the human self, the embodied nature of the self and a self that is 'cosmic and social' in origin, then questions about the realization of the universe, and communal and individual relationships with God are unavoidable. There is a need to move away from purely individual, disembodied eschatology and return to 'a unified individual, social and cosmic eschatology' (Lane 1995: 27).

The Body of Christ

One of the future tasks of body theology and an urgent one at that is the development of an embodied ecclesiology. What does it mean to the Church to be called to 'bodyforth' the revelation of God in Christ? What are the implications of seeking to live out an embodiment based upon baptism rather than biology? Is it possible for the Church to ground its ethics in the body while taking full account of the cultural construction of gender and sexuality? How is the Church to incarnate the love of a Trinitarian God dancing in an eternal mutual exchange of self-giving love, which is nevertheless deeply non-romantic in that it involves a mutual letting go into suffering and death on a cross? How does the Church as a body incarnate unitivity and hospitality? In an embodied ecclesiology liturgical practices, art and gesture would inevitably assume enormous significance and indeed perhaps would return to being the primary means through which beliefs are articulated, affirmed and proclaimed.

Jon Davies is highly suspicious of the whole body-theology enterprise. The body is surely a very fallible thing—mine is anyway—not capable of being either a moral agent or the basis of a new community—a community of everyone's bodies is likely to be a community caring for no one's body except as objects of exploitation and abuse, as objects of disunion (Davies 1997: 29). The obvious and inevitable difficulties of trying to place the body at the centre of theological discourse might well prompt the despair that Davies exhibits but this is a despair far exceeding those of his ancestors in faith. The Christian profession that the divine in all its difference has both created and entered into the ambiguity of human embodiment precludes such a despair. The body is indeed a 'fallible thing'. As the locus of divine revelation, it is established both as a point of contact with God and as a gulf of difference between the divine and the human, even as we touch the divine presence we lose her. This is the glory of the theological journey, it is what keeps us on it and prevents us resting for too long in shelters of our own making.

The human experience of embodiment is complex, ambiguous and diverse. It should come as little surprise, therefore, that theological reflection upon the body is all these things as well. What is remarkable is that both conservatives like Pope John Paul II and radicals like feminist and queer theologians are in agreement that 'the flesh is the hinge of salvation'.[6] This common starting point has the potential to produce the kind of creative dialogue that has largely been lacking in the Churches in recent years. What must be guarded against at all costs is the disappearance of the real, lived, laughing, suffering, birthing and dying body underneath the philosophical and theological meaning it is called to bear. It would indeed be foolish to allow 'the body' to become a disembodied entity.

6. Tertullian, *De resurrectione carnis* 8. 6-12.

Bibliography

Althaus-Reid, M.M.
  1997   'Sexual Strategies in Practical Theology: How to Plot Desires with Some
            Degree of Success', *Theology and Sexuality* 7: 45-52.
Amberston, C.
  1991   *Blessings of the Blood: A Book of Menstrual Lore and Rituals for Women*
            (Victoria, BC: Beach Holme).
Andolsen, B.H., C. Gudorf and M. Pellauer (eds.)
  1987   *Women's Consciousness, Women's Conscience: A Reader in Feminist Ethics*
            (San Francisco: Harper & Row).
Armstrong, K.
  1986   *The Gospel According to Woman: Christianity's Creation of the Sex War in the
            West* (London: Pan).
Badham, P.
  1976   *Christian Beliefs about Life after Death* (London: Macmillan).
Barth, K.
  1960   *Church Dogmatics* (Edinburgh: T. & T. Clark).
Beattie, Tina
  1997   'Carnal Love and Spiritual Imagination: Can Luce Irigaray and John Paul
            II Come Together', in Jon Davies and Gerard Loughlin (eds.), *Sex These
            Days: Essays on Theology, Sexuality and Society* (Sheffield: Sheffield
            Academic Press): 160-83.
Bell, R.M.
  1985   *Holy Anorexia* (Chicago: Chicago University Press).
Boff, L.
  1980   *Jesus Christ Liberator: A Critical Christology of Our Time* (London: SPCK).
  1987   *Sacraments of Life, Life of the Sacraments* (Beltsville: The Pastoral Press).
Borresen, K.
  1995   *The Image of God: Models in Judaea-Christian Tradition* (Minneapolis:
            Fortress Press).
Borrowdale, A.
  1991   *Distorted Images: Christian Attitudes to Women, Men and Sex* (London:
            SPCK).
Braidotti, R.
  1991   *Patterns of Dissonance* (Cambridge: Polity Press).

Brock, R.N.
1988   *Journeys by Heart: A Christology of Erotic Power* (New York: Crossroad).
Brooten, B.J.
1996   *Love Between Women: Early Christian Responses to Female Eroticism* (Chicago: University of Chicago Press).
Brown, P.
1988   *The Body and Society: Men, Women and Sexual Renunciation in Early Christianity* (New York: Columbia University Press; London: Faber & Faber).
Bunch, C.
1987   *Passionate Politics* (New York: St Martin's Press, 1987).
Butler, J.
1990   *Gender Trouble: Feminism and the Subversion of Identity* (London and New York: Routledge).
1993   *Bodies That Matter* (London and New York: Routledge).
Bynum, C.W.
1982   *Jesus as Mother: Studies in the Spirituality of the High Middle Ages* (Berkeley: University of California Press).
1987   *Holy Feast and Holy Fast: The Religious Significance of Food to Medieval Women* (Berkeley: University of California Press).
1991   *Fragmentation and Redemption: Essays on Gender and the Human Body in Medieval Religion* (New York: Zone Books).
1995   *The Resurrection of the Body in Western Christianity, 200–1336* (New York: Columbia University Press).
Camporesi, P.
1987   'The Consecrated Host: A Wondrous Excess', *Fragments* (Milan:, Garzanti).
Chambers, E.K.
1954   *The Mediaeval Stage*, 1 (London: Oxford University Press).
Christ, C.
1979   'Why Women Need the Goddess', in C. Christ and J. Plaskow (eds.), *Womanspirit Rising* (New York: Harper & Row): 273-87.
Chung Hyun Kyung
1990   *Struggle to Be the Sun Again: Introducing Asian Women's Theology* (New York: Orbis Books; London: SCM Press).
Coakley, S. (ed.)
1997   *Religion and the Body* (Cambridge: Cambridge University Press).
Comstock, G.D.
1993   *Gay Theology Without Apology* (Cleveland: The Pilgrim Press).
Congregation for the Doctrine of Faith
1986   *Letter to the Bishops of the Catholic Church on the Pastoral Care of Homosexual Persons* (London: Catholic Truth Society).
Countryman, W.
1989   *Dirt, Greed and Sex: Sexual Ethics in the New Testament and their Implications for Today* (London: SCM Press).
Cox, H.
1969   *The Feast of Fools* (Cambridge, MA: Harvard University Press).

Daly, M.
    1978   *Gyn/Ecology: The Metaethics of Radical Feminism* (Boston: Beacon Press; London: The Women's Press).
    1985   *The Church and the Second Sex* (Boston: Beacon Press).

Davies, J.
    1997   'Sex These Days, Sex Those Days: Will it Ever End?', in J. Davies and G. Loughlin (eds.), *Sex These Days: Essays on Theology, Sexuality and Society* (Sheffield: Sheffield Academic Press): 18-34.

Doriani, D.
    1996   'The Puritans, Sex, and Pleasure', in A. Thatcher and E. Stuart (eds.), *Christian Perspectives on Sexuality and Gender* (Leominster: Gracewing; Grand Rapids: Eerdmans): 33-51.

Douglas, M.
    1966   *Purity and Danger: An Analysis of Concepts of Pollution and Taboo* (London: Routledge & Kegan Paul).

Eco, U.
    1980   *The Name of the Rose* (London: Secker & Warburg).

Eiesland, N.L.
    1994   *The Disabled God: Toward a Liberatory Theology of Disability* (Nashville: Abingdon Press,).

Eilberg-Schwartz, H.
    1995   'God's Body: The Divine Cover-Up', in J.M. Law (ed.), *Religious Reflection on the Human Body* (Bloomington: Indiana University Press): 137-50.
    1997   'The Problem of the Body for the People of the Book', in T.K. Beal and D.M. Gunn (eds.), *Reading Bibles, Writing Bodies: Identity and the Book* (London and New York: Routledge): 34-55.

Eliot, T.S.
    1963   *Collected Poems: 1909-1962* (London: Faber & Faber).

Faludi, S.
    1992   *Backlash: The Undeclared War Against Women* (London: Vintage Books).

Feinberg, L.
    1996   *Transgendered Warriors: Making History from Joan of Arc to RuPaul* (Boston: Beacon Press).

Foucault, M.
    1977   *Discipline and Punish: The Birth of Prison* (New York: Vintage Books).
    1978   *The History of Sexuality. I. An Introduction* (New York: Random House).

Fox, M.
    1981   *Original Blessing: A Primer in Creation Spirituality* (Santa Fe: Bear and Co.)
    1987   *The Four Paths of Creation-Centred Spirituality* (London: CCS).

Gatens, M.
    1991   'A Critique of the Sex/Gender Distinction', in S. Gunew (ed.), *A Reader in Feminist Knowledge* (London: Routledge).

Gibellini, R.
    1987   *The Liberation Theology Debate* (London: SCM Press).

Gilhus, I.S.
    1997   *Laughing Gods, Weeping Virgins: Laughter in the History of Religion* (London and New York: Routledge).

Gilligan, C.
1982   *In a Different Voice: Psychological Theory and Women's Development* (Cambridge: Harvard University Press).

Goldenberg, N.R.
1987   'The Return of the Goddess: Psychoanalytic Reflections on the Shift from Theology to Thealogy', *Studies in Religion/Sciences religieuses* 16: 37-52.

Goss, R.
1993   *Jesus Acted Up: A Gay and Lesbian Manifesto* (San Francisco: HarperSanFrancisco).

Goudy, J.C.
1991   'The Sacraments', in Lisa Isherwood and Dorothea McEwan (eds.), *The A–Z of Feminist Theology* (Sheffield: Sheffield Academic Press): 209-10.

Griffin, G., M. Hester, S. Rai and S. Roseneil
1994   *Stirring Street: Challenges for Feminism* (London: Taylor & Francis).

Gutierrez, G.
1979   *A Theology of Liberation* (London: SCM Press).

Halkes, C.
1991   *New Creation: Christian Feminism and the Renewal of the Earth* (London: SPCK).

Hallman, David G.
1994   *Ecotheology: Voices from South and North* (Maryknoll, NY: Orbis Books).

Halperin, D.M.
1995   *Saint = Foucault: Toward a Gay Hagiography* (Oxford: Oxford University Press).

Hampson, D.
1990   *Theology and Feminism* (Oxford: Basil Blackwell).

Haraway, D.
1990   'A Manifesto for Cyborgs: Science, Technology and Socialist Feminism in the 1980s', in L. Nicholson (ed.), *Feminism/Postmodernism* (London: Routledge): 191-229.

Hardy, D.W., and D.F. Ford
1984   *Jubilate* (London: Darton, Longman & Todd).

Harrison, B.W.
1985   *Making the Connections: Essays in Feminist Social Ethics* (Boston: Beacon Press).
1990   'The Power of Anger in the Work of Love: Christian Ethics for Women and Other Strangers', in A. Loades, *Feminist Theology: A Reader* (London: SPCK; Louisville: Westminster/John Knox Press).

Harvey, G.
1997   *Contemporary Paganism: Listening People, Speaking Earth* (New York: New York University Press).

Heyward, C.
1989   *Touching Our Strength: The Erotic as Power and the Love of God* (San Francisco: Harper & Row).
1995   *Staying Power: Reflections on Gender, Justice, and Compassion* (Cleveland: The Pilgrim Press).

Hitchcock, T.
  1996 'Redefining Sex in the Eighteenth Century', *History Workshop Journal* 41: 73-90.

Hite, S.
  1993 'Women as Revolutionary Agents of Change', in *The Hite Reports: Sexuality, Love and Emotion* (London: Sceptre)

Hunt, M.
  1991 *Fierce Tenderness: A Feminist Theology of Friendship* (New York: Crossroad).

Irigaray, L.
  1985 *This Sex Which is Not One* (Ithaca: Cornell University Press).

Isherwood, L., and D. McEwan
  1993 *Introducing Feminist Theology* (Sheffield: Sheffield Academic Press).
  1996 *An A–Z of Feminist Theology* (Sheffield: Sheffield Academic Press).

Jackson, M.
  1994 *The Real Facts of Life: Feminism and the Politics of Sexuality 1850–1940* (London: Taylor & Francis).

Jagger, A.M.
  1983 *Feminist Politics and Human Nature* (Ottawa: Rowan & Allanheld).

Jantzen, G.M.
  1995 *Power, Gender and Christian Mysticism* (Cambridge: Cambridge University Press).

Jeffreys, S.
  1990 *Anticlimax: A Feminist Perspective on the Sexual Revolution* (London: The Women's Press).
  1994 *The Lesbian Heresy* (London: The Women's Press).

John Paul II
  1980 *Familiaris Consortio* (London: Catholic Truth Society).
  1981 *Original Unity of Man and Woman: Catechisis on the Book of Genesis* (Boston: Daughters of St Paul).
  1995 *Letter of Pope John Paul to Women* (London: Catholic Truth Society).

Jordan, M.
  1997 *The Invention of Sodomy in Christian Theology* (Chicago: University of Chicago Press).

Kolakowski, V.S.
  1997 'Toward a Christian Ethical Response to Transsexual Persons', *Theology and Sexuality* (6): 10-31.

Kristeva, J.
  1982 'Semiotics of Biblical Abomination', in idem, *Powers of Horror: An Essay in Abjection* (trans. Leon S. Roudiez; New York: Columbia University Press): 90-112.

Kuschel, K.J.
  1994 *Laughter: A Theological Essay* (London: SCM Press).

Kwok Pui-Lan
  1994 'The Future of Feminist Theology: An Asian Perspective', in U. King (ed.), *Feminist Theology from the Third World* (London: SPCK; New York: Orbis Books).

Lane, D.A.
  1995 'Anthropology and Eschatology', *Irish Theological Quarterly* 61: 14-31.

Laqueur, T.
 1990   *Making Sex: Body and Gender from the Greeks to Freud* (Cambridge, MA: Harvard University Press).
Lebacqz, K.
 1994   'Love Your Enemy: Sex, Power, and Christian Ethics', in L.K. Daly (ed.), *Feminist Theological Ethics: A Reader* (Louisville: Westminster/John Knox Press): 244-61.
Long, A.
 1991   *In a Chariot Drawn by Lions* (London: The Women's Press).
 1994   'The Goddess Movement in Britain Today', *Feminist Theology* 5: 11-39.
Lorde, A.
 1994   'Uses of the Erotic: the Erotic as Power', in J.B. Nelson and S.P. Long-fellow, *Sexuality and the Sacred: Sources for Theological Reflection* (London: Mowbray).
Loughlin, G.
 1998   'Sexing the Trinity' partly reproduced in *New Blackfriars* 79: 18-25.
         'Symbolic Waters', *Scottish Journal of Theology* (not yet published).
Louth, A.
 1997   'The Body in Western Catholic Christianity', in S. Coakley (ed.), *Religion and the Body* (Cambridge: Cambridge University Press): 111-52.
Lunn, P.
 1993   'Do Women Need the GODDESS: Some Phenomenological and Socio-logical Reflections', *Feminist Theology* 4: 17-38.
MacDonald, D.L.P.
 1995   *Transgressive Corporeality: The Body, Poststructuralism and the Theological Imagination* (New York: SUNY).
McDaniel, J.B.
 1989   *Of God and Pelicans: A Theology of Reverence for Life* (Louisville: Westminster/John Knox Press).
McDannell, C., and B. Lang
 1988   *Heaven: A History* (London: Yale University Press).
McFague, S.
 1993   *The Body of God: An Ecological Theology* (London: SCM Press).
 1997   *Super, Natural Christians: How We Should Love Nature* (London: SCM Press).
Malina, B.J.
 1996   *The Social World of Jesus and the Gospels* (London: Routledge).
Martin, E.
 1989   *The Woman in the Body* (Milton Keynes: Open University Press).
May, M.A.
 1995   *A Body Knows: A Theopoetics of Death and Resurrection* (New York: Continuum).
Merchant, C.
 1980   *The Death of Nature, Women, Ecology and the Scientific Revolution* (San Francisco: Harper & Row).
Miller, A.
 1988   *The Drama of Being a Child* (London: Virago).

Mollenkott, V.R.
    1993   *Sensuous Spirituality: Out From Fundamantalism* (New York: Crossroad).
Moore, G., OP
    1992   *The Body in Context: Sex and Catholicism* (London: SCM Press).
Moore, S.
    1996   *God's Gym* (New York: Routledge).
Morrison, T.
    1987   *Beloved* (New York: New American Library).
Nelson, J.B.
    1988   *Embodiment: An Approach to Sexuality and Christian Theology* (Minneapolis: Augsburg).
    1992a   *The Intimate Connection: Male Sexuality, Masculine Spirituality* (London: SPCK).
    1992b   *Body Theology* (Louisville: Westminster/John Knox Press).
    1995   *Power, Veiled Desire: Augustine's Writing on Women* (London: Darton, Longman & Todd).
Pittinger, N.
    1979   *The Lure of Divine Love* (Edinburgh: T. & T. Clark).
Plant, Judith
    1989   'Towards an Ecological-Feminist Theology of Nature', in *Healing the Wounds: The Promise of Ecofeminism* (Merlin).
Power, K.
    1995   *Veiled Desire: Augustine's Writing on Women* (London: Darton, Longman & Todd).
Primavesi, A.
    1991   *From Apocalypse to Genesis: Ecology, Feminism and Christianity* (Tunbridge Wells: Burns & Oates).
Prokes, M.T., FSE
    1996   *Toward a Theology of the Body* (Edinburgh: T. & T. Clark).
Pryce, M.
    1996   *Finding a Voice: Men, Women and the Community of the Church* (London: SCM Press).
Raphael, M.
    1996   *Thealogy and Embodiment: The Post-Patriarchal Reconstruction of Female Sacrality* (Sheffield: Sheffield Academic Press).
Rich, A.
    1977   *Of Woman Born: Motherhood as Experience and Institution* (London: Virago).
Robinson, J.A.T.
    1952   *The Body: A Study in Pauline Theology* (London: SCM Press).
Rudy K.
    1996   '"Where Two or More are Gathered": Using Gay Communities as a Model for Christian Sexual Ethics', *Theology and Sexuality* 4: 81-99.
    1997   *Sex and the Church: Gender, Homosexuality and the Transformation of Christian Ethics* (Boston: Beacon Press).
Ruether, R.R.
    1989   'Towards an Ecological Feminist Theory of Nature', in Plant (ed.), *Healing the Wounds: The Promise of Ecofeminism*.

1995   'Ecofeminism and Healing Ourselves, Healing the Earth', *Feminist Theology* 9: 51-62.
1996   *Women Healing Earth* (Harmondsworth: SCM Press).
Sanders, E.P.
1993   *The Historical Figure of Jesus* (Harmondsworth: Penguin Books).
Scully, J.L.
1998   'When Embodiment Isn't Good', *Theology and Sexuality* 8.
Sedgwick, E.K.
1990   *The Epistemology of the Closet* (Berkeley: University of California Press).
Segundo, J.
1976   *The Liberation of Theology* (New York: Orbis Books).
Seidman, S.
1992   *Sexual Politics in Contemporary America* (London: Routledge).
Selby, P.
1997   *Grace and Mortgage: The Language of Faith and the Debt of the World* (London: Darton, Longman & Todd).
Sheldrake, R.
1981   *A New Science of Life: The Hypothesis of Formative Causation* (Los Angeles: J.P. Tarcher).
Shiva, V.
1986   *Let Us Survive: Women, Ecology and Development* (Delhi: Sangapsh).
1988   *Staying Alive: Women, Ecology and Survival* (Delhi: Kali Press for Women).
Springer, S., and G. Deutsch
1981   *Left Brain, Right Brain* (San Francisco: Freeman).
Stone, M.
1982   'The Three Faces of Goddess Spirituality', in C. Spretnak (ed.), *The Politics of Women's Spirituality* (New York: Doubleday).
Stringer, M.
1996   'Are We Really Breaking Free?', *Reviews in Religion and Theology* 3: 15.
1997   'Expanding the Boundaries of Sex: An Exploration of Sexual Ethics After the Second Sexual Revolution', *Theology and Sexuality* 7: 27-43.
Stuart, E.
1995   *Just Good Friends: Towards a Lesbian and Gay Theology of Friendship* (London: Mowbray).
Swimme, B., and T. Berry
1992   *The Universe Story: From the Primordial Flaring Forth to the Ecozoic Era—A Celebration of the Unfolding Universe* (New York: HarperCollins).
Teilhard de Chardin, P.
1959   *The Phenomenon of Man* (New York: Harper & Row).
1960   *The Divine Milieu* (New York: Harper & Row).
Thistlethwaite, S.
1989   *Sex, Race and God: Christian Feminism in Black and White* (New York: Crossroad; London: Geoffrey Chapman).
Tillich, P.
1951–63   *Systematic Theology I–III* (London: SCM Press).
Tong, R.
1989   *Feminist Thought: A Comprehensive Introduction* (London: Routledge).

Trible, P.
  1987   *God and the Rhetoric of Sexuality* (Philadelphia: Fortress Press).
Tripp, D.
  1997   'The Image of the Body in the Formative Phases of the Protestant Reformation', in S. Coakley (ed.), *Religion and the Body* (Cambridge: Cambridge University Press): 131-52.
Vasey, M.
  1995   *Strangers and Friends: A New Exploration of Homosexuality and the Bible* (London: Hodder & Stoughton).
Walker, A.
  1982   *The Colour Purple* (New York: Harcourt Brace Jovanovich; London: The Women's Press).
Walton, H.
  1994   'Theology of Desire', *Theology and Sexuality* 1: 31-41.
Ward, G.
  1998   'The Erotics of Redemption: After Karl Barth', *Theology and Sexuality* 8: 52-72.
Ware, K.
  1997   '"My Helper and my Enemy": The Body in Greek Christianity', in S. Coakley (ed.), *Religion and the Body* (Cambridge: Cambridge University Press): 90-110.
Webster, A.R.
  1995   *Found Wanting: Women, Christianity and Sexuality* (London: Cassell).
Welch, S.
  1985   *Communities of Resistance and Solidarity: A Feminist Theology of Liberation* (Maryknoll, NY: Orbis Books).
West, A.
  1995   *Deadly Innocence: Feminism and the Mythology of Sin* (London: Mowbray).
Westermann, C.
  1974   *Creation* (London: SPCK).
Whitehead, A.N.
  1929   *Process and Reality* (New York: Macmillan).
  1938   *Modes of Thought* (Cambridge: Cambridge University Press).
Williams, W.L.
  1992   *The Spirit and the Flesh: Sexual Diversity in American Indian Culture* (Boston: Beacon Press).
Wilson, N.
  1995   *Our Tribe: Queer Folks, God, Jesus and the Bible* (San Francisco: HarperSanFrancisco).
Wolf, N.
  1991   *The Beauty Myth: How Images of Beauty are Used Against Women* (London: Vintage Books).
Woodhead, L.
  1997   'Sex in a Wider Context', in J. Davies and G. Loughlin, *Sex These Days: Essays on Theology, Sexuality and Society* (Sheffield: Sheffield Academic Press): 98-120.

INDEXES

INDEX OF REFERENCES

OLD TESTAMENT

INDEX OF AUTHORS

CPSIA information can be obtained at www.ICGtesting.com
Printed in the USA
LVOW07s1704230914

405487LV00003B/93/A